Additional praise for *The VC Field Guide*

"Venture capital investors aggregate a number of data points as they deploy capital in high-risk startups: Management teams, market problems, market timing, and more. In this book, VC William Lin has simplified the investor's diligence process by sharing his succinct and crisp framework, thereby simplifying a complex and opaque part of the VC business."

—Mahendra Ramsinghani, founder of Secure Octane Investments and author of *The Business of Venture Capital*

The VC Field Guide

THE VC FIELD GUIDE

FUNDAMENTALS OF VENTURE CAPITAL

William Lin

WILEY

Published by John Wiley & Sons, Inc., Hoboken, New Jersey.

Published simultaneously in Canada.

For general information on our other products and services or for technical support, please contact our Customer Care Department within the United States at (800) 762-2974, outside the United States at (317) 572-3993 or fax (317) 572-4002.

Wiley also publishes its books in a variety of electronic formats. Some content that appears in print may not be available in electronic formats. For more information about Wiley products, visit our web site at www.wiley.com.

Library of Congress Cataloging-in-Publication Data is Available:

ISBN 9781394180653(Hardback)
ISBN 9781394180660(ePDF)
ISBN 9781394180677(ePub)

Cover Design: Wiley
Cover Images: © cako74/Getty Images

SKY10044636_032023

Contents

Foreword

I've known Will for half of his life. We first met as mere fresh-men at UC Berkeley—both of us were undeniably nerdy, incredibly ambitious and wanted to truly make an impact on the world after graduation. Most of the students I met were studious, hard-working, and remarkable at consuming vast amounts of knowledge in a quick time frame. However, I knew right away that Will was different. Perhaps it was his unconventionally independent childhood or the fact that he had to chart his own path from a very young age without much familial influence, but the way he viewed the world was just different.

He was a natural problem-solver, very inquisitive, and intellectually curious about how the world works, and had the uncanny ability to see things that others didn't—he did that by transforming the data in front of him to create abstract ideas and frameworks that were scalable and applicable to a broad set of use cases. Once he solved a problem in front of him, he instantly began to codify the framework behind how to solve 100 versions of those problems in the future. He enjoyed building things that could transcend beyond him and naturally helping as many people that came in his path.

So when I heard that he was writing a book about a framework for how to evaluate investment opportunities, I laughed. Of course. As a fellow venture capitalist myself,

I often get asked the question: why did some VCs invest in the Zooms and Squares of the world and others didn't? How did the VCs have the foresight that these companies would be so successful? And why did so many VCs pass on the initial investments in these companies? As much as we can codify exactly why these amazing VCs were able to pick Zoom and Square at the early stage and realize their immense potential before anything was obvious, the reality is that a large chunk of it was due to luck. And the other chunk of it was due to that "gut feeling."

But what exactly informs that gut feeling? Is it possible for that gut feeling to evolve over time, learning from pattern recognition across other investment opportunities and the osmosis of being in the industry? This is Will's primary thesis—while this book won't give you the answers of yes or no on a particular investment opportunity, it'll help provide you with the fundamentals on how to develop that "gut feeling" with an insightful framework on what to evaluate and focus on when looking at a new investment opportunity.

Venture capital has always been an exclusive industry—for every company that a VC funds, they'll likely end up passing on 1,000+ companies. But how do they arrive at these decisions? How are they able to adjust their risk tolerance for some companies and not others? This framework will serve as a good starting point to help illustrate how to evaluate an investment opportunity and develop a better "gut feeling" over time. It'll finally democratize the decision-making behind an industry with so much mystique and allure.

Priya Saiprasad,
Partner @ Softbank,
Life Partner to Will Lin

Preface

Growing up, I remember feeling a conflicting mixture of emotions every day for my parents—grateful for them shipping me off to the United States when I was 5 so that I could have an American education, but resentful of them not being there for me as a role model. As an adult now, however, I've become only grateful as that experience shaped me into who I am today. It forced me to figure out how to navigate life and American culture first-hand and, if I was lucky, find role models: people that I admire, respect, and could learn from. It turned me into someone who loves to see the world from another perspective.

In the early days, I wondered what it was like to have easy access to role models at home. People who could help me with my homework, deal with bullies, and talk about classic schoolyard dramas. I continue to believe that I'm lucky to have a career at all. I still look back on my life and see all the ways I was likely to fail. Honestly, if so many lucky breakthroughs hadn't perfectly lined up, who knows what I would be doing today? So whenever someone genuinely helped me, it left a deep impression and I still remember them to this day. This includes the many mentors I've had since then, in college and so far in my career.

I wrote this book because of my mentors and the help I've received over time. While my career is far from being over and this may sound like I am about to retire, I wanted to take a moment to share what I've learned with others interested in the often misunderstood and opaque world of venture capital. My goal is to "demystify" and explain venture in simple terms (hence the title), using a framework I've found valuable when working with founders and their companies. This book is not meant to be the ultimate compendium on how to succeed in venture, fund the next dozen decacorns, or land on the Midas List tomorrow, but a straightforward and personal perspective on this profession from someone who has been in it for over a decade.

I hope it helps underscore why I spent years, at nights and weekends, working to get this book over the line. It's to help that person who is determined to make their next breakthrough but unclear on the how. No matter how much mentoring and coaching I try to do, none of that scales compared to getting information onto pages, into a book, and in people's hands.

So I do feel privileged to have the opportunity to write this book and share my candid thoughts about the venture capital ecosystem. While I know this book will not answer every question or answer everything definitively, I hope you will find it useful. This book is filled with perspectives that I already regularly share in my communities and with more content that I could ever deliver over hours of in-person coaching.

Thank you for reading this book. Stay in touch. Ping me or ask me questions on LinkedIn: www.linkedin.com/in/linwilliam. Tell me when this book helps and even when it doesn't. Life is a rollercoaster.

William Lin

Acknowledgments

Thank you for helping me to be a better investor, entrepreneur, and passable writer: fellow board members, team members, community-builders, and early book reviewers.

Priya Saiprasad

Lin family

Saiprasad family

Adnane Charchour

Adrian Sanabria

Alberto Yépez

Alex Konrad

Alex Pinchev

Allan Alford

Amit Pandey

Andrew McClure

Anne Marie Zettlemoyer

Andy Cao

Arneek Multani

Barmak Meftah

Bill Carroll

Brian Castagna

Brian Markham

Byron Alsberg

Casber Wang

Charlie Giancarlo

Chris Bishko

Chris Castaldo

Chris Jones

Chris Olsen

Chris Roberts

Chris Wenner

Christina Richmond

Connie Qian

Dave Zilberman

David Endler

David Tsao

Deepak Jeevankumar

Don Dixon

Don Duet

Enrique Salem

Eric Quanbeck

Erik Bloch

Ernie Bio

Evan Wolff

Feng Hong

Francis Brown

George Hoyem

Gerald Beuchelt

Gil Beyda

Guillaume Ross

Gustavo Alberelli

Gwen Castro

Helen Patton

Howard Ting

Howard Zeprun

In Sik Rhee

J. Ram

Jai Das

Jake Flomenberg

Jeff Shreve

Jilbert Washten

John Cowgill

John Moragne

John Steven

Jon Gelsey

Jon O'Connell

JS Cournoyer

Julie Albright

Karl Sharman

Katherine Walther

Koos Lodewijkx

Leo Casusol

Lisa Lee

Lucinda Rhys

Manoj Apte

Marc Talluto

Mercy Caprara

Michael Biggee

Mike Hluchyj

MJ Ramachandran

Mohit Tiwari

Nipun Gupta

Owen Van Natta

Paul Lanzi

Pete Birkeland

Priscilla Kawakami

Raj Dodhiawala

Raj Judge

Rajiv Sinha

Rakesh Soni

Rey Kirton

Rita Gurevich

Rob Ackerman

Rob Fry

Ryan Naraine

Sam Haffar

Sarah Ashburn

Satish Dharmaraj

Scott Crenshaw

Sean Cunningham

Shane Shook

Sheck Cho

Shobie Ramakrishnan

Sid Trivedi

Sinan Eren

Sounil Yu

Srikant Vissamsetti

Steve Huffman

Sue Chung

Tamara McCarthy

Tanya Loh

Thomas Luciano

Tim Keeler

Todd Algren

Todor Tashev

Tushar Kothari

Uma Reddy

Vincent Liu

Yoram Snir

Part I

Introduction

Introduction

MY BACKGROUND

I still remember the state of the economy when I graduated. It was an important time for me. Interviewing for my first real job out of UC Berkeley felt like the culmination of all my education and life preparation—and at that point, the economy was a bloodbath.

I remember high-achieving graduates having their prestigious offer letters rescinded after already proving themselves during summer internships. Brilliant people who could not find alternative options because employers had already made all their entry-level hires. I remember record unemployment and so many students going back to live with their parents, jobless, and unsure how they were going to pay off their student debt. I saw how that experience turned my entire graduating class into risk-averse working professionals pursuing careers in the highest-paying, lowest-risk, and tried-and-true jobs available out of college.

Meanwhile, I didn't have a home as a fallback. At that point I couldn't go back to my childhood home in Salt Lake City, Utah. Everyone I had lived with had moved away. My standard operating model was already to "figure it out." I have lived without my parents since I was 5 as a first-generation immigrant. I had a lifetime of being different and I had no idea what to call my experience until the pejorative term, "anchor baby" was popularized on the news.

For my graduating class, that highest-paying tried-and-true job in business was investment banking. Only a small number of students were able to break into it, and in the midst of record unemployment, we were incredibly grateful for the opportunity to work 100+ hours a week. My first year in investment banking started with providing investment banking services for financial institutions like AIG, Metlife, and Cigna and then a second year for technology companies like Facebook and GoPro.

Venture capital is seen today as one of the most visible careers in finance, making headlines with each startup unicorn ($1 billion+ valuation) milestone. It has been the genesis for some of today's most successful companies like Google, Airbnb, Instagram, and many other startups that are now household names.

During my time in banking, as my peers moved to tried-and-true roles at private equity firms and hedge funds, I stubbornly pursued a career at the intersection of entrepreneurship and emerging business. I was one of the few candidates to both interview and receive an offer at a venture capital firm in 2012. I joined Trident Capital, an enterprise-first VC with specializations in adtech, business services, cybersecurity, and healthcare IT. I joined the cybersecurity team as an associate and that's where I met Alberto Yépez and Don Dixon, the core group I would work with for the next decade, first, at Trident Capital and then at our spin-out to create the sector-focused Forgepoint Capital, a leading VC firm with its roots in cybersecurity.

Over this decade the economy picked back up and, with it, a shift from risk-averse thinking to risk-tolerant investing. This led to an exponential growth in venture capital over the past decade as well. While I have had the chance to work with many aspiring venture capitalists (VCs), I've also seen many fail to make it a long-term career. These are hard-working, smart, motivated people with all the right credentials and skillsets. It doesn't make sense: they are incredibly bright and capable, and every bit as deserving as me or more. So what happened?

I've wondered if it's because they've struggled with something that frustrates me too and was actually one of the biggest inspirations to write this book in the first place. When I first started in venture, I didn't have any frameworks or background, so in my early career, I had to hit a lot of dead ends in order to finally piece things together. Sure, there were random books that addressed financial models and the tactical aspects of being a good investor. Perhaps you could read VC blogs for specific insights but it's not like anyone sits you down and says "This is how it works" in simple terms. So this book is my attempt to do just that. I hope this guide and the Venture Capital Investment Framework (VCIF) help others learn from my mistakes in order to aid their own journey through the murky maze of venture capital.

As I reflect on where I am at this point in my career and its challenging beginnings, I am grateful for having taken the path I did and feel lucky for what I was able to learn and do as a result. I was one of a handful of people who got to work with one team, to start from the bottom and work my way up through the ranks. Simultaneously, I helped to build a venture capital firm from the ground up. I've gotten to see first-hand how to found a successful VC firm, from raising the capital to establishing the team, the strategy and the investment approach, to making the investments and working with exceptional entrepreneurs to build thriving companies.

Throughout, I've had the opportunity to observe senior, experienced people across multiple venture capital firms make decisions, and I've worked with and learned from brilliant mentors over the years—yet, amazingly enough, none of these opportunities guaranteed my success in the VC industry. Same goes for so many others who have tried to make it in VC.

Venture is still very much an apprenticeship industry that is mentor-led yet requires a self-driven mindset. You have to do a lot of self-education, learn by doing, and get up to speed quickly. What happens when you work with seasoned investors who are experts at what they do is that by simply watching them, hearing the questions they ask and taking note of the approach they take, you develop an understanding for what they see as important. You come to understand how they try to rationalize key decisions in order to persuade all parties of what they believe to be the best path forward. You end up using your powers of perception to pattern-match and figure out why they felt positive about one discovery, and negative about another.

Because of the nature of on-the-job mentoring, you can't expect busy VCs to describe exactly what's going on while they're being pulled in multiple directions. That just doesn't scale because each mentor has multiple mentees, they serve on multiple boards and have to look after their portfolio companies, and, on top of that time commitment to mentoring, they have firms to manage. Mentors are not classically-trained teachers or coaches who make the learnings or plays explicit—that's not how mentorship works, especially in venture. The opportunity for a person new to the industry is to be in the same room, to see the same data as a senior investor, to help digest the data in the style the senior investor thinks is the best format, and then to gradually build the credibility to help influence the decision the team makes.

I'm one of those mentors in my community. I enjoy spending time investing in people, whether I am helping someone choose between multiple job offers, working with founders to make critical decisions, creating qualified win-win connections between opportunity and talent, suggesting skills that will position someone for their next step, or helping them foretell what the decision-makers are considering behind the scenes. To be good at this requires that I understand, enjoy, and, over time, build empathy for almost every type of role within the startup ecosystem.

The common theme across our ecosystem is that everyone follows their respective learning curves by doing, by trying, sometimes succeeding, sometimes failing, and always learning from those various experiences. They need exposure to startups, perhaps by investing in their careers and joining or founding a startup, by investing their budget and purchasing from a startup, or maybe by investing either their own capital or their investors' capital in startups or venture capital firms. If they were lucky, they made informed decisions and learned from the decisions with the help of a mentor or advisor.

Unfortunately, many people never get the opportunity to get exposure to venture capital, let alone develop deep mentor relationships.

Despite all that exposure to experienced investors and rapid company growth, making money-losing investments is still expected: it's common for 20% or more of venture capital invested to go to zero (called "venture capital loss ratios").[1] This is almost the exact opposite model of the leveraged buyout (LBO) private equity model where the priority is investing in a company that can capably and predictably pay down the debt on their balance sheet. For traditional LBO private equity, loss ratios are significantly lower.

With so much risk in venture capital, that means that the winning investments are rare and impactful. Everybody wants to know, why did you invest in a successful company X, Y, or Z? Attend any panel about venture capital featuring any successful VC and they always get asked why they invested in a particular company that hit a major milestone or exited. This is because there is a lot of room for interpretation about what makes a great opportunity.

For example, almost every mega-successful founder will have dozens of stories of how they pitched their ideas to VCs and were rejected exponentially more times than they were accepted, especially in their riskiest and uncertain early stages. Today, we look at the success of Uber and say, "Of course, I would have invested in that," but would you have done so in 2009? Riders trusting their life with a perfect stranger at the wheel—who knew? Only a few people invested: they embraced the idea and risk, and believed it would be possible to change consumer behavior to create a viable, sustainable service and business model that would be reliable, safe, and profitable one day. The decisions investors and venture capital firms make are often difficult to understand.

Even after being in the industry for a while and listening to my peers, the decision-making process is individual across the board. Not everyone has the same reasons for investing or passing on a startup. It took me a while to listen to all these people, study my own decision-making process and realize there is still structure to how people make decisions—it's just not verbalized, not readily shared. The reality is, even after a decade, this industry moves so quickly that thoughtful decisions at one time can quickly become brilliant or silly at another time.

That brings me to one of the biggest inspirations to write this book: my own frustration and struggle in understanding venture. When I started out, I didn't have any frameworks or a background, so I hit a lot of dead ends in order to piece things together. As I learned from watching others and fumbled around gaining professional experience, I kept asking myself: "How do these great VCs make their decisions? What really matters to them?" I liked VC firms' slogans like "people first," "protecting the digital future," or "companies of consequence"—but what does that actually mean in practice?

This book introduces the Venture Capital Investment Framework, which is designed to help consolidate my and your learnings into a pattern to venture capital, prompt what I believe are productive questions as you learn, to fill in blanks, and to humanize and put some sort of structure around some of the qualitative aspects in venture that are challenging to measure. When I was starting in this industry, I searched for a framework, or a cheat sheet, but I couldn't find one. I can't tell you why that was the case, but the most reasonable answer is that it is still a relatively young and mentorship-driven industry. So for the next generation of VCs, entrepreneurs, and investors, the most important way to progress was, and still is, to learn by doing.

What we've seen across multiple industries, however, is that each generation is able to learn faster than their predecessors, thanks to the power of information. So while I didn't have a framework to encapsulate the lessons I've had to learn over the past decade, I hope the following helps further the continued evolution of this dynamic, exciting, and interesting industry and career path for those who choose to pursue it.

WHO IS THIS BOOK FOR?

The aim of this book is to provide exposure to the art and science of entrepreneurship, working with startups, and to reveal the inner workings of venture capital. I do a fair amount of mentoring and networking and the common theme I've heard is that the people who want to get into venture capital (aspiring investors) or participate in the ecosystem (as founders, limited partners, customers embracing emerging tech, etc.) often have the least access to it.

So whether you're a founder, a startup employee, a student, a rising venture capitalist, a customer of startups, a public market investor, a corporate development leader, a lawyer, a consultant, an investment banker, a business unit lead, a private equity investor, or a limited partner—or a multiple of the above, or generally curious, this book is for you.

Because finance and venture capital are full of acronyms and specific terminology, I've included a glossary at the end of the book. One term to highlight is "Next-Gen VC," which applies to investors early in their career and it helps to differentiate the people who have decades of experience.

As a Field Guide, I have organized this book to help readers pinpoint the areas they'd like to focus on, whether that's fundraising, board dynamics, etc., although it's entirely possible to read the book from start to finish. In the remainder of this Introduction I discuss the genesis of the Venture Capital Investment Framework. How did I come up with the framework and what problems does it help solve? I follow that up in Part II where each chapter explains a different component of the Venture Capital Investment Framework. In Part III, I explore venture capital for specific audiences and stakeholders, such as students, current VCs, entrepreneurs, limited partners, and startup customers.

THE FRAMEWORK'S ORIGIN

Access to knowledge has always been a catalyst for change, whether it is a simple disagreement up to empowering humanity to evolve across arts and sciences. It also has the potential to provide perspective and accelerate growth but the issue has always been the same. We aren't born with knowledge and have to learn it. So the first and biggest obstacle for anyone who wants to better understand VC is gaining access to this knowledge, access to this experience, access to being able to see the ins and outs of venture first-hand.

When I first became a VC, I struggled to make sense of the industry because, unlike a lot of consulting or finance firms, venture capital firms are typically small and they don't have an onboarding process, they don't have a lot of training or knowledge forums, and you are expected to hit the ground running and learn by experience. When I started out, I didn't know anything about the industry and my thoughts were, what the heck is this industry? What do people do? How do they make the decision to invest in one company and not another? What due diligence do VCs carry out and what do they look for in an entrepreneur or in a startup? When they're saying, "Hey, I want to invest in this company," what questions are they asking? Who are the great venture capital firms and why are they great? Where does the money come from? How does the transaction, the matchmaking, come about and how do the entrepreneurs and the VCs find each other? How do they decide what the terms are to work together? There are so many questions that I had, that I didn't understand, and if you were to ask me in my early years in venture capital how these important decisions are made, I wouldn't have been able to tell you why one deal happens and another doesn't.

Even though I had access, I didn't have the answers. I struggled to figure out simple things, like what is right and what is wrong. Just because something happened, like a company failing miserably, how do I understand what happened in the postmortem? There are so many different potential hypotheses on how and why something happened and it's not like we have these parallel universes to look into and conclude, "Oh, in this universe, X happened and in a different universe, Y happened." We just don't have that. And so, as a result of so many of these experiences—both good and bad—whenever I sat down to draw out the key lessons learned, I was never happy that the lesson was grounded in enough data or was unbiased based on my own preferences. I didn't yet understand what was truly happening beneath the surface and why.

There was no formula, there was no structure to figuring out why some investments went well and others failed. I spent a lot of time guessing, "Oh, yeah, we didn't have the right set of leaders at this stage of the company, or the product was ahead of its time, or the company was solving a problem that ended up not becoming a real big problem, or the team didn't scale." Unlike in science or any analytics role, why a startup is or isn't successful cannot be rationalized via a multivariate regression or even simple A:B testing. Not only is there no standard way to adequately compare companies, there is no defined way to even measure the data.

As a result of constantly struggling in venture in my early years, I decided that, to be successful, I needed to develop an approach based on the scientific method for myself. How could I make sure that I learned as much as possible, given the unique access I had? I started going through VC and entrepreneur interviews, going to conferences, listening to hundreds of recordings of successful people, and then I applied my own experience to all of it. Initially, it was just a flood of information and I tried to capture as much information as humanly possible and make sense of it all later. I referred to this process as "turning over rocks," a phrase one of my mentors taught me.

What does turning over rocks mean? It refers to the required work to make a comprehensive decision. To leap into a new project knowing little, to turn over many rocks that yield nothing on the other side or even worse, bad news. To sometimes not know exactly what you are looking at and having to guess something is good or bad. To have to pause making a decision until other rocks are turned over and connecting the dots. It also refers to the importance of prioritization and experience. As you gain more experience, the ability to prioritize also grows. Yes, you will turn over every single rock, but is it possible to look at every rock and guess what is on the other side? To find the higher-priority rocks first? Eventually, with experience and data, it becomes possible to "see the matrix". To be able to see the common patterns and turn over rocks effectively.

As I gained more experience in venture, that ability to knowledgeably turn over rocks was glorious. Having my own point of view led to more confidence and willingness to speak up during group decisions knowing that my insights were rooted in data and experience. I was hungry to better learn how VCs outside of my team made decisions. It eventually led me to start asking hard questions to fellow VCs: "What process did you take to do this?" "What did you learn?" That's what led to the next phase of starting to hear the common keywords: Team, TAM and sometimes Tech or Timing. The "Three Ts." It was then that I started to understand that there was an unofficial way to evaluate companies beyond the financials. Even knowing that the three T framework existed, I still didn't feel confident and I didn't know if it was good enough. I saw something, I believed something, but is that enough? Can I stop? Have I reached a bar that I needed to reach in order to feel like this is an "A" team? My gut says, "Yeah, this makes sense, that's good," but is it enough? One reason that a lot of leading-edge industries struggle is that they don't have a way to measure success and, without that, sometimes you just spend more and more time and effort turning over rocks. I hope to remove a bit of that struggle with this framework, which is what I consider to be the six most important questions to ask. This framework is the amazing result of diverse thinking in the VC ecosystem and means that each person can have different fundamental questions and success criteria per question.

ENDNOTE

1. Fred Wilson has a nice post about loss ratios in his blog series, AVC; https://avc.com/2013/11/loss-ratios-in-early-stage-vc/. Also look at wlin@forgepointcap.com for targeted results.

Part II

The Venture Capital Investment Framework

1

The Venture Capital Investment Framework

STARTUP INVESTING

The relationship between an entrepreneur and their venture capitalist (VC) is a lot like the relationship between a player and a coach. The VC/coach typically has a broader perspective because they meet lots of companies, sit on a lot of boards, and learn from multiple entrepreneurs'/players' experiences while studying the market and analyzing the gaps. At the end of the day, the entrepreneur decides what the company will do, motivates the team, and executes it on the field. With that in mind, venture is a unique ecosystem where people have to work together. No one party holds all the cards and no one party can dictate the terms, so all parties have to make their own decisions on who they want to work with. If a startup is going to be successful, if it's going to be profitable, scale, and endure, then VCs, entrepreneurs, startup employees, and startup customers have to be aligned—which is a lot easier said than done. With this Venture Capital Investment Framework (VCIF), I hope to help innovators in the startup industry: VCs, the entrepreneurs and founders creating companies, the startup talent, and startup customers who work in or with the companies, and folks aspiring to be any of the above in the entrepreneurial ecosystem.

In my experience, startup investing is still an imprecise art. Venture capitalists tend to either highly productize their process— we are talking complex spreadsheets or software programs quantifying each little detail—or essentially wing it based off vibes. Both can work. But it amuses me, and doesn't surprise me, if a useful framework like this would be helpful medicine for both.

(Alex Konrad,
Senior Editor @ Forbes covering
venture capital, cloud, and startups)

The following are what I consider to be the most important questions in VC. I believe these provide a simple yet effective way to arrive at the fundamental answers needed to confidently streamline the decision-making process and to work with a startup. These questions actually mirror a framework we've used since Aristotle's time: Who, What, When, Where, Why, and How. These are great questions to ask before starting or working with a company, much less investing in one. Aristotle's framework still exists for a reason: after years of learning and figuring out that, if you really want to understand something, you need the answers to those six questions.

I have organized the book to cover each of the questions and explain how they apply to venture. This will show you how you should structure your thinking, and the related questions you'll want to address to make those decisions in the startup ecosystem.

Chapter 2: Who = Team
Chapter 3: What = Problem
Chapter 4: When = Timing

Chapter 5: Where = Market
Chapter 6: Why = Solution
Chapter 7: How = Scale
Chapter 8: How to Use the VCIF

I remember when I first encountered questions that fit in these six categories. In the initial days, I didn't even know why those questions mattered. I just wanted to know the answers. But all of these questions need your point of view when you carry out due diligence on a company. So, for example, you'll want to get to know the team, understand them, know their strengths and weaknesses. And the same for the product: what is it? What does it do? What problem does it solve? How important is it? How valuable is it? For "Where," the question is, how big a market is this? "When" involves timing and is critical to startup success. "Why" gets at product management, around customer empathy, and the solution. How well do you understand your customer? The "How" identifies the concept of scale—is the company changing and improving as the other factors change and improve? Does the company have the right resources to be able to continuously evolve alongside the customers? One important component here is the sales machine, which has plenty of KPIs to measure success.

When you first start with the framework, it might feel like a lot of guesswork, but as you get comfortable with the six questions, it will become second nature, especially as the answers become clear from more exposure to entrepreneurs and startups. This doesn't mean because everyone is using the same framework that they'll all come up with the same questions or answers. Why have multiple partners in a VC firm if everyone is going to have the same questions and answers? You want that diversity of thought and you want those different perspectives because it makes organizations better. Sometimes having diverse opinions and ideas can lead to a longer decision process, but usually the more diverse the people and their perspectives, the better answers you get.

If you take ideas about the team, everyone is going to have different ratings. For me, I love curiosity in a team but someone else might hate that and say that all they care about is mental horsepower. They look at a team where everybody has straight A's in every single class they've ever taken in their entire life, and they say, this team is going to be super-successful. Someone else is going to say, nope, I did not get good grades—I'm only looking for drive. So everyone is going to apply that "team" part of the framework differently and that happens because we're humans, we're all unique, we all have different childhoods, different life experiences, and different things that we're wary of. But yet, there's still some structure in terms of human behavior and we have spent a lot of time trying to figure out those structures. We all know about the Myers Briggs or the Big Five type personality tests. And, for me, I think those are very productive, very helpful, because they help you start making sense of the world. It's a framework mindset, a systems approach to understanding people.

For me, I grew up thinking everyone's a secret, super-special snowflake—everyone is different; everyone is unique. And if you think about someone like a VC who is trying to work with a large number of people in their career, they're never going to be able to understand every perspective. They're always going to have to learn about a person for the first time as if it's a brand new person and they would have no prior experience to apply to this person because they don't know them at all. But

with frameworks, I can think, "okay, you are an introvert. I know how to work with introverts. Oh, you're an
extrovert. Okay. I know how to work with extroverts."
Yes, there is some generalizing that I'm doing. There are
16 people patterns in the world according to the Myers
Briggs, which seems low—but are there more than 300
different types of people in the world, personality-wise?
I'm an introvert so I don't naturally enjoy certain situations but a big part of being successful is building and
expanding the network of people to help me source
deals, triage business ideas, hire CEOs, or pull off a strategic acquisition. I had to find the introvert's way to networking and building relationships to progress in my VC
career. While it took time for me to learn, I didn't have to
find a rare unique way of doing things, there were plenty
of introverts in the world that I could learn from.

With this framework, now we have six categories of
things to sort data into. One of the dynamics of venture is that
you're never going to get every single question answered.
Venture is inherently risky and there's no perfect information. But this framework gives me the confidence that I've
applied my experience and I've done my due diligence in a
programmatic and structured way. And whatever decision
I make, I did it as thoughtfully as I could.

Does Order Matter?

Do you know the feeling that sometimes things are
just meant to be? While realizing the "most important
questions" that I've learned to ask in VC are the Who,
What, When, Where, Why, and How framework, another
important coincidence made it the perfect guide for VC:

even the order of the framework aligns with the milestones a startup needs to achieve as it matures.

- Who = Team-Fit (can this founding team work together well?; Pre-seed stage).

- What = Team-Problem Fit (is this team a good fit for the problem?; Seed stage).

- When = Timing-Problem Fit (has the team proven the "why now?"; Series A stage).

- Where = Market-Problem Fit (what is the size of this problem and what long-term strategy makes sense?; Series B stage).

- Why = Product-Market Fit (does their product solve the market need and how well?; Series C stage).

- How = Scale-Market Fit (has this company scaled appropriately to keep up with the market demands to eventually reach IPO?; Series D and later).

If you're already familiar with VC, the next chapters jump into my interpretation and some of my learnings related to each section of the VCIF, but if you're new to the industry or need a refresher or more context on where the framework comes from, the "Notes to Stakeholders" in Part III can be helpful. There I share additional opinions, thoughts, and advice for specific stakeholders in the entrepreneurial ecosystem, the innovators and creators, the investors, the customers, and anyone who may want to pursue a career in this ecosystem.

2

Who = Team

The team is one of the first things VCs focus on and it's critical for a startup's success. Many VCs have been CEOs themselves and VCs just love their CEOs they love them. They embrace the golden rule: treat others as one wants to be treated. They know exactly how to work with CEOs, they know what makes a CEO great and they'll quickly assess a team and CEO and say things like, "This is a scenario where I see this CEO will shine. This person is an 'A Player.'" What about the successful investors who've never been CEOs?

I find it helpful, when assessing a team, to start with pattern matching based on my experience with things I've seen in the past. "Pattern matching" is a common phrase in VC conversations and what it means is taking prior experiences that are similar and applying those to a current situation—it's a shortcut, a way to distill lots of information into something recognizable to you. And that prior experience doesn't have to be a 1-to-1 correspondence to the situation because there is a lot you can learn about a team from personal experience—yours and theirs. And because everyone is unique, everyone will have different patterns that emerge for them.

You might find a pattern from a high school coach you had, or a musical director; you might have a pattern based on a teacher or a neighbor or your first job selling ice cream at the local carnival. It could be anything, but it's a pattern that emerges for you based on what you're seeing from a startup team. So, for example, suppose you are talking with some founders and you think, "I've seen the beginning of this pattern before," and what you remember is that it ended in some result—either positive or negative. You think it could happen again with these founders, or a version of that could happen again. You still have risk in assessing a team because there's no perfect information, but pattern matching helps to highlight the important things out of the countless things you could be considering.

I had a ton of assumptions about what team meant when I was starting in this industry. But after being on multiple boards and seeing multiple companies, I began to look at the successes and failures and spent a lot of time thinking, "Why did this team do well or not so well?" The big part of the experience for me, and for other VCs as well, is that it's so common when something isn't going well to blame the team. You invest in a company that has a lot of promise, but if they're not achieving what you thought they would be able to achieve, the classic, human response is finger-pointing. When things aren't going well, it's not my fault, it's your fault, it's someone else's fault, right? And because of this classic, almost knee-jerk reaction, it's common to blame the team when things don't go well. But here's the thing: the nature of a startup is that things aren't going to go well all the time. It's guaranteed that the companies you invest in will have their moments, good and bad. It is impossible for all to be successful all the time. There are always going to be ups and downs, even along the path to becoming a successful company. When things are rough, a lot of investors, especially if they're earlier in their investment journey, will also feel disappointment and think, "Ugh, I wish I didn't have to invest time and effort into this team."

The finger-pointing is not unique to VC—it's a common management lesson and people apply it to all sorts of things beyond business. School system failures, law enforcement response failures, traffic accidents, in nearly any "failure" in society that happens we tend to place the blame on people. We often talk about success and failure falling on the shoulders of one person. But it's also true that one individual can completely change the direction of an organization. Look at all the coaching changes in professional sports—and it works, sometimes. In our society, our businesses, our organizations, everything goes really well when there are good leaders who take responsibility because the buck stops with that person, and we know exactly who to both celebrate for successes, but also who to blame for failures. And the person who takes on that leadership role also takes on both credit for successes and blame for failures. As a result, the team becomes such a critical component to any investment we make, but to be able to evaluate a team, you need to understand yourself.

What I mean is that you must understand what biases you might have that can impact your assessment of a team. For example, we all have different friends—not just the same friend, and the reason we all have different friends is because we have different preferences. The same is true with teams. There is variety in each VC's experience, background, and biases that come into play and that's why some VCs love a particular team while others would completely avoid it. Some VCs love aggressive CEOs white others prefer CEOs who are collaborative, easy to work with, kind, and friendly. The other dynamic when you're assessing a team is to understand leadership styles. All of these can impact the success of the startup, but the important thing is that there are a lot of ways to succeed, not just one.

In my experience, as a self-proclaimed "nice guy," I've always feared that the "nice guys finish last" dynamic was something that was fundamentally true, but luckily, in reality, it isn't. That was one bias that I needed to break through. When I grew up, society celebrated Steve Jobs, for example, who was known for his brilliant and belligerent personality. He was not an easy person to work for. And you've likely heard the same thing about famous CEOs like Mark Zuckerberg, that he was not an easy person to deal with, either. And because there were plenty of famous data points like that, I worked to get myself comfortable with the idea that the most successful CEOs were either difficult to work with or eventually became difficult. I was wrong about that. People are not so black and white. There are a lot of really nice people who are successful as well and there are lots of different versions of success, so focusing on things you really like or really dislike is not that productive, right? There is not one path to success.

DIFFERENT PATHS TO SUCCESS

There are many different pathways to success and the team is obviously important in determining which to take and how to get there together. There is a framework that is beautifully aligned to a path a company naturally takes. In venture, you'll commonly hear the term "product-market fit." It's used both to talk about a successful company ("Hey, this company has achieved product-market fit") and also to talk about failures, like a company failed because it didn't have product-market fit. Actually, before product-market fit there is "founder fit": Do the founders work well together and do they work well with each other? And right after founder-fit is team-problem fit: Is this a team well situated for the problem that they're tackling; do they have the vision, plan, and skills that complement each other and deliver what's needed for the problem? If not, how do you augment what they have with additional resources? After the team-problem fit, startups need to figure out the timely solution, they need to figure out what is relevant now, build it, and sell it.

A lot of people immediately jump to product-market fit and make a decision about whether or not they want to work with a company or invest in it, but product-market fit is down the line: startups need to have founder-fit, team-problem, and a product before they get to product-market fit. The initial stages I mentioned are about founder-fit and team-problem fit and similarly, in my framework, team and people are the beginning. There is really nice alignment between the stages of the company and this framework. The first question is, what are the criteria that people should think about when they think about evaluating teams? This question will come up in your first meeting with a startup or, you will be thinking about how you can help take this company to the next level. If it's not already a rocket ship or an A grade company, you'll be thinking how you can help make it one. Or you could have a B grade company where you think that they could become A grade with a little bit of help. You could potentially find a technical founder, or their first salesperson or the first marketing person.

CURIOSITY IS A MUST-HAVE FOR FOUNDING TEAMS

Wonder is the beginning of wisdom.

—*Socrates*

In my personal experience, when I look at very success-ful teams and very successful founders, the key criterion that really makes a difference is curiosity. Curiosity is, for many, many reasons the one must-have in a founding team because entrepreneurship is inherently a learning game. As an entrepreneur, you, everyone who's been in this industry and everyone who is trying to build something in this industry, are all doing things that they haven't done before. There is so much experimentation that's required to be in the startup world, and that means there has to be a lot of self-learning and self-improvement for each team member and founder. Without curiosity, without the self-drive to keep on improving, it's very difficult to succeed in a startup. So curiosity—not college degree, not experience, not skillset—is the key to being successful in entrepreneurship. No matter what your preference, whether you love the aggressive, difficult personalities or you want to work with those super-nice, easier personalities, no matter what, all those people, especially if they're working for a startup, should be curious.

You might think that's well and good, but how do you know if someone's curious? If you ask a person about curiosity, they'll most likely say that they are curious, since that's a positive attribute. But how do you know? The questions you ask aren't specifically to test a person's curiosity but to learn more about them, the team, and the company. The way to figure out if someone is curious is to listen to how they answer certain questions. For instance, a classic example of how they answer, that might demonstrate curiosity, is how they talk about lessons learned. When a person says they learned something, or they tried something and figured out a solution, or they had a big surprise or a big flop—those are all signs of curiosity. Normally when we think about curiosity, we think about books people are reading, podcasts they're listening to, or other ways of absorbing information. That's great, but in a startup there isn't enough information and there aren't easy resources. The best way you can learn in a startup is by experimenting, by taking steps and either succeeding or failing and learning along the way.

Another proxy for curiosity can be gleaned from a person's role within the early stages of their startup. The reality is that everyone has many different responsibilities, especially in the earliest stages of a company. People are handling different tasks and spanning workloads far beyond what they would in more mature organizations, which can be both exciting and exhausting, but helpful for startups that internalize and share the learnings to accelerate growth. The salesperson might be doing a little bit of finance, the engineer might be doing a little bit of customer success, and the CEO might be doing a little bit of everything—janitorial work included. People in startups need to take on different roles. The breadth that comes with doing different things, of having experience across many areas, is very beneficial. So the first proxy is whether or not people take on roles outside of their comfort zone, and the second is, are they actually enjoying the role and trying to learn more about it? In the early days, it is a lot easier to improve and grow and learn as an individual and being focused on only one thing is often a detriment. For example, if you're in sales and one day you would like to be VP of Sales or Chief Revenue Officer (CRO), knowing about marketing, finance, customer service—all of the parts that impact sales—will serve you better in the long run. And the only way to be good at all of these things is to do them in an early-stage company and that happens because a person is curious and knows how to channel that curiosity into productive forward progress.

INDIVIDUAL OR COMPANY GROWTH?

One of the challenges for nearly everybody in a startup is the tension between individual growth versus company growth. I have seen this so many times now, where a company grows faster than an individual's skills that may be required to keep up. Take, for example, the sales rep who really wants to be CRO one day. They may have started when the company had five account executives, then, boom, the company grows like a rocket ship and pretty soon they have expanded from a small and mighty sales team to a matrixed organization of a hundred sales reps. It is virtually impossible for that sales rep to immediately become the CRO of a hundred salespeople in the short timeframe the company took to go from 5 to 100 sales reps.

Is this a bad thing? No necessarily. The aspiring sales rep gets to learn from others who join above, around, and below them. Meanwhile the company can hire an experienced person to be the VP of Sales and fill in those gaps, someone who has experienced those learnings before. The experienced VP who comes in can immediately step in and fill in that gap of what the company needs and what the team has. Boom. Now that new VP of Sales has to grow, too, as the company expands into new markets and verticals. Then the pattern could repeat: the company continues growing and needs a SVP before the VP of Sales could grow into the role. The company might then add another sales leader and a CRO above that, triggering commentary among the venture community such as, "They're replacing their head of X, Y, or Z, every year, 18 months, or two years because the company is growing so quickly."

There's also the flip side, where the individual grows way faster than the company. When this happens, that's when people move on to new opportunities. Especially for the folks who are super-curious, super-achievement-driven, and want to keep improving in their careers. If the company doesn't grow at their pace, they quickly come to the realization that, "Okay, it's getting hard for me to learn here, so time for me to move on." There is also a common dynamic where the company isn't growing and new leadership roles aren't being created. This results in a ceiling for top-performers and high potential talent who should be rising in the ranks but cannot because someone else is frozen in their seat. Early-stage startups need to be very mindful and accept turnover if their employees outgrow the company or if the company is not growing enough to promote people to roles with greater responsibility and learning.

THE CEO AND TEAM CHALLENGES

One of the challenges that some startups have is placing team over company. That's a very common growing pain with a company and I can argue both sides on this one. The reason why it happens is the reality that a leader can only spend time with a certain number of people and they usually spend most of their time with their direct reports. The most effective way for a CEO to push the company in the right direction is through culture, principles, and leading through example. The culture helps set who a company hires, what type of working style the company will have, what communication style they want, what their values are, and so on. That's the best way for the CEO to really help drive the company. As a result of the CEO's limited time to interact with everyone, there are people who are going to be in the inner circle and those people are going to have more information, more insight, more knowledge of the strategy, than others. The folks who are not in the inner circle will inherently feel like they are disadvantaged in multiple ways, both in terms of information, in terms of career prospects, maybe even in terms of engagement, motivation, and passion. As a leader, it is very difficult to try to make sure lots and lots of people are in the inner circle because there is a lot of work that's required to achieve that. A way around that limitation, and what we see in a lot of early-stage companies, is for the CEO to become a historian of the company. They're constantly talking about the history of the company (e.g., why we did this, why we did that, how we picked out our logo, etc.) and that helps to reinforce the culture and explain to the folks who aren't in the inner circle what the heck is going on within the company as well. And so there is a natural organizational behavior limitation placed on the CEO in particular, and C-suite people, too, because people only have so much time.

Placing team over company might make it easier to overcome limitations, given the size, scope, and speed of a company, but it can also lead to bad decisions. For example, sometimes leaders have a recency bias so when their inner circle is saying, "Hey, this is really important," that sticks in the CEO's mind. They just heard it, it had just blown their mind and they're thinking, "Wow, this is really important," and it takes them off the track from what's actually important for the company. For example, suppose a CEO hears that the company should experiment with a new business line that sounds really interesting and seems really complementary, and multiple people within the inner circle just told the CEO that it was important. The CEO responds, "This is important, I'm going to go do it." But it turns out that it's not such a good idea and the new business line ends up failing, which wastes time, money, and resources—as well as possibly tarnishing the company's reputation.

The other problem in startups is not promoting talent who have a lot of promise into the inner circle. Sometimes, as you know, it's really difficult for a founder to fire someone who is in their circle for someone else who might be better at that job, because the team has all this history, memories, and friendship. So there are a lot of challenges with the team in a startup.

CURIOSITY AND. . .?

A lot of the challenges that a startup will throw at you are impossible to anticipate as a first-time founder, which is why curiosity is an important must-have for founding teams. Beyond curiosity, the other attributes that VCs look for vary across the board, but it's important (to me) that whatever skills and attributes founding teams have are complementary skills aligned with curiosity. It's really important to hire folks who have been excelling and achievement-driven throughout their lives, because by hiring these overachievers, you know that they're going to have access to all this knowledge. They're going to have the curiosity to pursue that knowledge, and they're also going to have the track record to keep growing within the company as well.

Specialization

You might ask, how you know whether someone is achievement-driven, smart, or not, and I can't judge that. I can only guess at that. But you can look at their prior achievements as only one proxy. The other thing I place value on in an individual in a founding team is a desire to specialize in something, because if you want to progress within your career as an individual contributor (growing into a manager and then a leader), then specialization is critical. By specializing, you can become the best of the best at something. And when we think about a company from the CEO's perspective, they are thinking about people so that they can fully delegate engineering to someone, and fully delegate sales to someone else. This leads to a scenario where every CEO wants to delegate to someone who's the best of the best at that. And so specialization is what helps you become the best of the best at it, and that's what helps you progress within your career.

Being a generalist is a luxury. Most of us generally rise within our school systems as generalist students. However, eventually, we enter the working world that naturally asks for specialization. If you want to receive more responsibilities and rise within the career ladder, you have to earn them with your capability. Responsibilities require you to improve yourself, to gain new skills and to become a reliable source of valuable, differentiated results. It requires you to become an expert at something and potentially among the best of the best. That specialization journey is what eventually makes you more unique, difficult to replace, better compensated and eventually to a stable point where you can enjoy the luxuries of being a generalist again. To be able to pursue passions outside of your specialty.

If a founding team is not curious, then it's a showstopper, and as a VC, I'd just move on. It doesn't matter how talented they are, how novel their product is, or how smart they are, because, to me, entrepreneurship is all about learning and curiosity at the end of the day. But if that curiosity does exist, then we next start to look at team dynamics, which is a little bit more subjective to what may sound outright judgmental.

For instance, VCs can rate teams as A, B, or C as a shorthand for who they like or dislike, but there's no true definition of A, B, or C. One attribute of a team that's not subjective and is really important is their ability to sell—whether that's the ability to sell themselves, their idea, their solution, or their vision. "Selling" is critical for startups and founders. A lot of early teams and founders don't know how to sell and that is a detriment on multiple sides, not only in terms of the customers, but in terms of hiring, too. Someone who can't communicate well and stumbles or struggles, or someone who doesn't know how to answer questions with customers, that's bad. But what's also bad is they can't hire either, because if you can't sell to your customers, you can't sell to great A-player employees to join you. Some people in the industry think of sales ability as a nice-to-have. but, for me, it is a must-have. And the ability to sell is a learned skill—I am an introvert and I learned how to sell, so it's a skill that you can develop over time. In fact, I'm still learning and practicing how to sell in some way in a completely different way now as a startup founder.

Culture

When you think about culture, you think about it in terms of scale. You don't think about it in terms of happy-go-lucky feelings, or everyone is a friend. You think about it in terms of a leader of an organization and the problem you're faced with is: how do you scale the team in terms of their human needs? Because as a leader, at some point, you cannot be friends with everyone in your organization.

At some point, you can't have conversations with everyone in your organization. At some point, you have no idea what someone is doing, you don't know their name, you don't know anything about them. And that happens because you don't have enough time in the world to have these one-on-one relationships. The question becomes, how do you scale your organization despite that restriction? And the solution that most leaders gravitate toward is culture.

Culture is what helps set decision-making processes and values on how you will operate. For example, a culture can be a "disagree and commit" culture where you want everyone to argue with each other, debate to no end, and then eventually commit to a decision together and decide to come together and move on. Or a culture can be highly collaborative where all decisions are made as a group and everyone has to agree, or maybe you have a majority rule that you use to make decisions. There are cultures where, if you don't have unilateral support of something, you don't even do it. You just skip it.

Every organization has their own culture and culture comes from the top, the criterion comes from the leadership team. When people gush about organizations, they gush about the processes that are inspired by the culture. So, for instance, Amazon has their key values and one thing they talk about is the one-way door and the two-way door and that's the way that Amazon thinks about decisions. A one-way door means that if a decision is something you cannot revert out of, let's spend more time thinking about that decision, and a two-way door means, if you can make a decision but you can back out of it, then make a decision and let's move on. The one-way, two-way door idea is not something in just one part of Amazon, it's company-wide and it is driven from the top.

Culture plays a huge role in the success of a company, but you need to look at that in the form of the leadership team and how much they understand the importance of culture and whether they have clarity on their vision for the culture they want to set.

FAILURE IS A VALUED ASSET

There are some things that immediately stand out to VCs, for instance, whether a founder is a multi-time entrepreneur. That's important because there is confidence that a multi-time entrepreneur has already learned many hard lessons from their previous startup(s). A multi-time entrepreneur will avoid some of the mistakes they made before and they will have more of a running start than a first-time entrepreneur. That's very factual and something that people value. It doesn't have to be a unicorn exit and it actually doesn't even have to have been a successful previous exit. One of the counterintuitive things that VCs look at is failure; it's one of the things that VCs focus on.

For a long time, Silicon Valley celebrated failures in terms of failed startups. And that is a very valid, very worthy measurement, because one critical thing that multi-time founders can do is build their team a lot easier. Not only can they build it easier, but hopefully they can build with people that they've already worked with and previously built trust and rapport with. And because you learn so much about a person once you start working with them, it's a little bit like dating. Similar to how you don't really know someone until you move in with them and you see them in a non-dating environment, you learn about their eating, sleeping, and exercise habits, or whatever it is, but you really learn about a person if you move in with them.

Similarly, in the world of startups, you don't really know someone until you start working with them and you go through the ups and downs together. In doing that, you learn how great they are, you learn what their strengths and weaknesses are, and in many cases it allows the company to scale quicker. And also the people that multi-time entrepreneurs hire are usually A-players because the founder is an A-player and A-players usually hire A-players, right? When you're hiring a lot of A-players to join the team, then other people will say, "Oh, wow, that's really awesome. This is like a rock star team. I want to be a part of it." It's infectious! And so that makes it easier to hire more A-players and build a high-performing company. So the benefits of having a multi-time founder extend beyond just avoiding mistakes, it also impacts the quality of the team they can put together.

There's another version of the multi-time founder which is really interesting as well, and that is when a founder comes in who was never a founder before but worked in another startup. Typically, folks who led sales, maybe marketing, maybe product management, people from those three functions can become really great founders and really great CEOs. In those cases, the more successful their prior startup, the better, because that means they got exposure to a lot of really interesting things as a company was growing. And even though they were heading sales, for example, and not leading engineering, they still saw how the engineering team had to grow to support the success of the company. They have an idea of what success looks like or what the milestones are, or what some of the pinch points are.

IN-PERSON DATA

The final advice for VCs on evaluating a team is that the best data still comes from face-to-face meetings. Yes, you can definitely look at their backgrounds "on paper" and that's a really nice objective way of trying to guess how good a person, team, or company might be. That's the beauty of LinkedIn because that platform provides everyone's background so easily and makes it accessible, but really you can't get to know the true potential of a team unless you meet them in person. Whether you are an aspiring VC or an entrepreneur working with a VC, the most important interactions occur in person; for an entrepreneur, it really comes down to asking the right questions and then answering the questions with the right answers and tone as well. Your goal as a VC with in-person meetings is to get a good sense of this person's ability in different scenarios. How are they going to act when they need to pivot? What are they going to do when they need to fire someone? Who are they going to ask for help when they miss their first quarter? This is also where the benefit of experience on both sides helps. As a VC, the benefit of our experience is that we've gotten to see multiple teams succeed and fail. Because we've seen so many iterations of both good and bad outcomes, we will ask questions to see how founders react. Take, for example, a thriving startup experiencing growing pains.

During fundraising, the founders state they intend to use the funds to scale up their team to better deliver their solution and expand in key markets. We will ask, "You have 30 employees now and you want to grow to a hundred employees. What are your key hires? Who are the key individuals you need to hire in order to hit 100 successfully?" If they don't say anything about finance, then we know this is an area for learning and improvement. The next thing we'll try is to coach them, to give them advice to see how they react. If it's a chore to advise them now, that's a red flag coaching them later won't get any easier. From experience seeing multiple companies, and understanding how important advice, feedback, and coaching can be to their success, if founders aren't open at all, then it's going to be really hard to coach them and help them be successful.

The team is the most scrutinized aspect of venture capital, but it's not the easiest thing to evaluate or assess. Asking questions that measure a person's curiosity and asking questions that beg for a reaction are two skills that will serve you well.

Sometimes the reason the team is so valuable is because, often, pivoting is the name of the game in the startup world. Let's say someone chose to create something where their timing is off—they're way ahead of the market. What do they do, wait years for the market to catch up? No, they pivot to something else. The platform Slack is a perfect example because it was a gaming company that pivoted to create a workplace communication software. Who do we give credit to for fixing that, for making that change? The team. The team did that and so a great team can ameliorate some of the other issues that impact success, like timing or market. If the market is a "C" and the team is an "A," they can still make great things and I have seen near unicorn exits of "A" teams in average markets. The team is important, especially in early-stage companies where they don't have enough traction to build up the operational part of their business.

TEAM DYNAMICS THAT WORK

There are a lot of approaches people take to evaluate startups but at the end of the day everything is measured in terms of results. Startups can fluctuate across a number of dimensions, such as revenue growth, profitability, how well they are managed or how healthy their team dynamics are, but at a high level, companies are measured by financial results. With all that variety in venture capital, with all that variety in building businesses, it's difficult to evaluate start-ups. There just isn't a lot of data available. But I have two examples of teams that have done incredibly well—they have done almost everything that I hoped they would do, which is to manage their profitability well in the context of their growth. And I wanted to describe both of them because they are very different from each other yet still incredibly successful. The two cases also highlight how much variety there is even with a framework like the VCIF.

The Team That Over-Delivers

One example of a team that I thought over-delivered in terms of what I think a team should be was a company that we invested in when they were at about 100 employees. And one of the key themes that enabled this team to be successful was that the company also had services roots versus product roots. The importance of that was they were able to manage the culture of the organization and they prioritized it. For example, they had weekly automated check-ins with the team and they asked people how they thought the week went, what the pluses and minuses were. They had regular checks with the entire organization about whether or not the company was following the key questions they wanted the company to adhere to. They had regular town halls where people could ask any question without embarrassment or retaliation.

That approach might seem like a minor deal but when you are a services company, you have to think, what's the most valuable part of the company? It's the people—the people who are delivering the services, selling the services, hiring additional services people, training them to be more successful, coordinating them. It's all about the people. For example, this company taught me—before the pandemic and before many organizations were fully remote—that if you have a meeting that's hybrid where some people are in the office and others are remote, you should make the whole meeting remote. The people in the office should go back to their individual desks and call in so that everyone on the call has the same experience of being fully remote. Because if you don't, the people who are in the office together and in one room end up prioritizing people who are in the room, and the people in the room have more of a voice and that's unfair and that doesn't foster a fully remote environment.

When I think about this company and I think about their superpower and their strengths, I think about the way that they treat their people, the way that they manage their people. And this is something that comes from the top—anything related to culture comes from the top. It is impossible to create a culture from the bottom logistically. I'm grateful to this company because they invited me to their offsites and I had the chance to experience the culture and see what it was like to be an employee of the company. And I understood why this company always gets these "best places to work" awards because they are a great place to work, and they have great people who are motivated, who are happy, who feel supported by their organization. And that translates into people delivering the best they can do.

Not every company is able to achieve this level of community or culture within their organization. It's not necessary, but I do think it is a superpower because culture streamlines a lot of other things as well.

The Team That is Strong Top-Down, Bottom-Up

The second example of a team that was incredibly strong was from a company where the CEO was able to hire C-level people at an early stage. Typically, C-level talent *might* be persuaded to join a 200-person startup, but this team had a deep bench of C-level talent when they had 30 people in the company and they stayed with the company a long time. I've seen highly qualified people, like a CRO, for example, who could lead gigantic teams but when they joined a startup as the first salesperson, they fail. It is a unique skill to be a leader of a function that could go from five people where you're the only person doing this function to being a leader and manager of a gigantic organization that reports to you. Generally, you find that once a person gets to a level where they have a 50-person team under them, they're not really excited to go back to being the only person doing the function.

A common phrase in VC is that, in the very early stages, you need to hire someone who is a player/coach, someone who's on the field playing but also able to coach and build a team. But what you often find is that as people become a coach, they usually want to stay a coach. They don't want to go back to being a player/coach. Of course, there are a lot of reasons why this happens and I wouldn't blame it on the individuals themselves. For instance, perhaps these early-stage companies couldn't even use all the value or couldn't even tap into all the value this person could offer them. Perhaps the company can't give them enough equity or doesn't have enough cash to pay the person the amount that they need to take on the job. I wouldn't blame it on the individual if a coach doesn't usually join a startup to take a player/coach job.

But this CEO was able to find people who were successful coaches and bring them into the company as player/

coaches. And that's remarkable because most people who are hungry for more responsibility and a more complex job at a much larger organization rarely join a startup as a player/coach. Because these people ended up being really great players/coaches and were able to continue to scale with the exact same organization, it was a hugely important reason why the company was successful. It's very common in startups that you have to up-level each role after a certain amount of time. Your original head of sales, for example, could be an amazing player and now you need them to be a player/coach and they can't do that. They just can't make that transition. Or now they're an amazing player/coach and you need them to be a coach and they can't make that transition. Or you've grown so large that the person is not even coaching a team anymore, now they're coaching teams of teams. And they can't make that transition.

For many startups, what happens is they need to keep up-leveling because it's very difficult to find people who are growing individually at the same rate that the company is growing. So how did this CEO get the individual and company growth to align so well? They hired people who were more experienced than the company really needed at that point in time but they were able to show these people that, "Hey, the company is going to grow quickly and even though you feel overqualified, you won't feel that for long." This was a company that was able to manage the company growth to individual growth incredibly well so that as the company continued to grow, the person who was in the seat as the leader of these functions was able to stay there. We didn't have to replace the CMO, we didn't have to replace the head of sales, we didn't have to replace the engineering lead. And that longevity is incredibly valuable. The reality is that most startups can't achieve this longevity because if you are a first-time entrepreneur, it's difficult to hire someone who is both perfectly qualified for the role and able to grow and stay with the company for a very long period of time.

The other really difficult thing that this company did really well was being able to calibrate whether a person was qualified, overqualified, underqualified, or whether this person was the right fit for the role. Very few people can do that calibration and this is where the experience of executive recruiters is helpful because they have completed so many feedback loops with candidates that they fit into jobs. There are also VCs who have exposure to that kind of data where they can say to founders, "Okay. I've seen this and I can apply my experience to help you decide whether or not this person is qualified, whether this person is a good fit for the company."

Ultimately, the only person who can determine whether or not a candidate is a good fit for the culture is the CEO. A good fit is someone that you, the CEO, wants to work with and vice versa—that person wants to work with the CEO or the entrepreneurs. This is not something a CEO can delegate to an executive recruiter, this is not something you can delegate to a VC and depend on their perspectives because no matter what, recruiters and VCs are external to the organization. No recruiter or VC will understand your company like you do, if you are the CEO. They are not in every single interview meeting with you. They don't know how the candidate is reacting, and they don't know your culture the way that you do.

And beyond skills and roles and individual growth aligning with company growth, culture fit is a scenario where, if things don't work out, there are many negative outcomes. One of the main ones is that when a person is not in a culture fit, they try to change the culture to their liking. Maybe they can do that and maybe there's a happy medium that

can be sustained for a time. But if it doesn't work to the level
they want, they get frustrated, they're unhappy, and then
they start poisoning the culture. They start being detractors
in the organization, start questioning every single decision,
and start harming the overall culture and overall motivation for other people working in the organization. Culture
fit is incredibly important because we all like the feeling of
moving forward, not backwards, and when we hire someone who is not a culture fit where they start poisoning the
organization, we are definitely feeling that we are moving
backwards. It's very painful. No one enjoys it.

3

What = Problem

In the "Who" (Chapter 2) I talked about founder-fit ("are these founders good fits with each other?") as a precursor to team-problem fit ("is this team a good fit for the problem?"), timing-problem fit ("is this a timely problem to solve?"), and product-market fit. It's nearly impossible to predict whether team-fit is a strength or weakness because the real tests happen when things aren't going well. It is nonetheless important to try to make sure that the things under your influence, like founder-fit and team-fit, are going well in the very beginning. The next element on this road to product-market fit is validating the problem. It's actually quite common for early-stage startups to fail to validate their initial problem.

Many founders I know were inspired by success stories like Steve Jobs, and marvel how he was seemingly able to predict customers' needs and delight them with innovative solutions over and over as the company grew. There's a common conception that these visionaries are recognized as some of the smartest people in the world and heralded as being able to build and delight customers with something that customers hadn't seen before and hadn't even thought of before. But unfortunately, this model doesn't work out that way very often and, even worse, when these same companies fail, so rarely do we get the opportunity to hear why they failed. Instead, we only hear about successful examples and that's what we remember and, in doing that, we have a selection bias of successful examples leading us to believe in a "build it and they will come" mentality.

What happens instead is that startups often build something they think is novel and clever and cool before truly understanding the problem that they are actually solving—not from what they believe to be true, but from their target customer's perspective. When you think about the common keywords in entrepreneurship, like product-market fit and ideal customer profile, what those are really focused on is having a very clear sense of the problem that you're solving. Having a very clear sense of the problem that you're solving makes everything else involved in building a startup so much easier. It makes building a team easier because you'll know what skills you need to fill it out. It makes figuring out sales easier, because you know which customers are more likely to have this problem and you'll be able to align your sales organization to the customers' needs. It makes fundraising easier, too, because VCs want to make sure that they don't make competitive investments. If founders have a very clear perspective of the problem, that helps a lot.

When the most successful VCs listen for the problem, they are not listening for the problem that you want to solve—they are listening to how you describe the problem, what you know about the problem, and how you think about the problem. Where did your data come from? Where is your gut pointing you toward as well? They are listening to your approach to the problem, rather than the problem itself, because those tiny nuances are fundamental to every action and every decision that this team is going to make in the future as they build their business.

I have heard stories about how top-tier VC firms approach pitches given by founders and they focus 100%

of their attention on each of those pitch presentations. They don't look at their phones, they don't have side conversations with others in the room. They are listening very, very carefully to the words to understand all the small nuances. Their goal during a pitching session is to figure out if this person truly understands the problem. If you're the "build it and they will come" person, you will have people thinking, "Yeah, this must be a problem," but is it actually a problem? For example, suppose a founder comes in and pitches something around laundry. We all do laundry so we would all probably like some innovation in laundry, such as a way to fold laundry. The founder hates folding their own laundry and would love to solve that problem, maybe coming up with a laundry folding machine. Is there a market for that? Will customers buy something like that? At what price point? So just speculating about a problem isn't enough, and what we run into in venture is that a lot of entrepreneurs enjoy thinking about problems that they understand and that they have exposure to, and then creating a solution for that problem. But without validation, it's just thinking about problems and coming up with solutions, you're not creating a viable business.

DEEP QUESTIONS, FIRST PRINCIPLES

It is much better to go five layers deep into the problem than to assume that because you have that problem, and there are a lot of people like you, that everyone wants a solution to that problem. A deep dive is not only about the problem, but also about who has this problem, and why does this problem even exist? Who all the different constituents are who are dealing with this problem also factors in, because it's usually not only your one customer that has a problem, it's usually your customer plus five other people. And so the question is, why are all of these people focused on this problem? How much budget is usually associated with this problem? Is it something that is already budgeted or do you have to create the budget for something like this? If it's a new laundry folding solution, that will probably be a new expense because the way people do it now is with their own labor.

I feel that Steve Jobs is a classic example of the "build it and they will come" mentality, and he was particularly influential for millennials. We experienced the iPod, the iPhone, the app store and each of those things were such delightful experiences that didn't exist before Apple, right? The reality is, they did exist before Apple. Prior to developing the iPhone, Apple tried doing the PDA thing, and before the iPod, there was obviously the Walkman. So, these innovations by Apple were not never-before-seen-in-the-world things, but what Steve Jobs and the Apple team did really, really, really well, was, they understood the problem. And by understanding the problem really well, they used those principles to design the right solution to that problem. If you make decisions based on the fundamental reasons why the problem exists, you can ignore what's already happening in the world. There is the classic Henry Ford quote, "If I had asked people what they wanted, they would have said faster horses." If you asked people in the mid-1800s, when everyone was riding a horse, what could be better than a horse, they would reply: a faster horse. But if you asked that same question in the mid-1900s, you'd get a different answer: a car. Who knows what everyone would ask for hundreds of years from now?

A decision based on first principles would ask, "What is the fundamental problem we need to solve?" and the answer is, we need to be able to get around, to be able to go places. That's the fundamental problem. It's not that the horses aren't fast enough or that a car solves every single transportation problem, because at some point in our future the car won't be the solution, either. It's critical for entrepreneurs to understand the problem and use first principles because this understanding drives the team and every underlying decision a founding team will make. Sometimes an entrepreneur will mention that they made a hundred calls with customers before even writing one line of code and what they are signifying is that they wanted to make sure they deeply understood the problem before doing anything. And that is such a great decision, especially in the early days of a startup, and something that I highly recommend. I wouldn't highly recommend to founders that they make the whole hundred calls just so they can say that they made a hundred calls, because it can be misused. You can always make a hundred calls and not ask the right questions, not be curious about the problem. There is a tendency for founders to keep selling their idea, even with potential customers, so they just keep pitching and selling rather than listening to customers about the problem.

One of the fundamental components of validating the problem is that most of the time, you can't just ask a customer what the problem is because they will give you a solution and what you need is multiple perspectives. That's the exact same scenario with the faster horse solution mentioned earlier. And the problem is, most people don't ask deeply about a problem, they don't approach it with curiosity so much as with confirmation about their own ideas. For example, suppose you ask a business unit leader about a problem in their organization and they say that they don't have enough visibility into everything that's going on within their domain. Furthermore, they tell you that if you, as a would-be entrepreneur, could give them visibility into their organization, that would be great—that would be something they would potentially buy. Most first-time founders will take that answer and run with it and say, "Absolutely! Let's go build this solution." But if you probe and dig deeper, you might ask questions. Why do you want visibility into that part of the organization? Why didn't you have visibility into that part of the organization beforehand? Who else wants visibility into this part of the organization? How could we potentially do this? What are the data sources that we would have to plug in to provide that visibility? There's so many of these deep questions to ask, and obvious follow-up questions, but when you're in startup mode and you are sprinting and you are trying to generate revenue as quickly as humanly possible, these questions don't get asked. And sometimes, people will make up what they think the customer will answer to those questions because they think it's common sense.

COMMON SENSE AND BIAS

We all have our own biases, everyone does, including me. We have our own lens that we use to give us a view of the world, and the customers have their own views of the world as well. If one customer tells you something, that's not nec-essarily what every single other customer would say, and the best entrepreneurs will use their natural curiosity to understand the nuances of what customers are saying. The best teams use their curiosity to tackle the depth around the problem they are validating, and in doing that, they will ask more and more questions. Even though it feels like you have more than enough information, it's always better to go very, very deep into the problem.

For founders, one thing that's common in startups is that in going deep on validating the problem, they realize that it's not really a solvable problem. Either they can't solve the problem, or people won't pay to solve the problem; either way, validating the problem nullified their business ideas. When this happens, startups will pivot to something different, but the success of that pivot depends heavily on the stage and flexibility of the company.

If you're a later-stage investor, the pivot is very hard to do at that point in time because the team, the operating systems and processes, and the customers are already there. So a pivot at this point is nearly impossible to pull off. However, for an early-stage company, the pivot is a lot easier. It's even better if a startup is still not spending a lot of money building a product when they pivot because that allows them to be very nimble. And that is actually a very common scenario, especially in the seed stages, where a phenomenal team comes to a VC and the VC says, "I really like where you're going, but I've been working on this other problem that's very adjacent, very close to what you're talking about right now. And this is my vision for what your company should do."

YOU DON'T HAVE TO SOLVE YOUR OWN PROBLEM

It may be surprising to hear there are stories of teams pursuing another idea after a conversation with a thoughtful VC, but it happens fairly often. In my experience, some of the best relationships between a VC and the founders happen because the founders have the opportunity to start working and see the value from the VC early in their life cycle. The reverse is true too: the VC has an opportunity to partner with, coach, and mentor a team really well because the team listened to them and took the advice of the VC early on. This goes a little bit back to the idea that everyone has different biases and preferences. Not every team is a perfect fit for every investor and there are many different versions of success. There isn't only one perfect team or one perfect idea, or one perfect VC. And not every problem can be solved.

There are problems that will always exist until the end of time. For example, we will always need to communicate with others until the end of time and the easier we make it, the better. There will always be improvements, and entrepreneurs who think deeply about the problem in the context of the current environment, in the context of timing, in the context of the team's capabilities, in the context of funding needed—they might be able to solve some communication problems. There are all sorts of key dynamics that have to be understood during the validation phase that it's easy for founders to miss some of the key ones. That's why a VC can be helpful to a startup, because as VCs we have the benefit of meeting many, many teams, we have the benefit of thinking very strategically and broadly about a range of problems.

Sometimes VCs will have a problem ready to go and then if a phenomenal team comes in, the VC can pitch their idea to see if they'll build the solution. This can happen when a founder is a multi-time entrepreneur and the team has worked together and knows exactly what their strengths and weaknesses are. They have achieved a certain amount of success, maybe a ton of success or maybe very little, but there's the dynamic of working together. The classic definition of an A team is that the team is still hungry. Maybe they built a business and they sold it for $200 million and the founder made $20 million and while most people will say, "That's a lot of money, I'm done," for an entrepreneur, that might not be enough to satiate their professional aspirations. They are not going to stop there; they are not going to retire. They are going to aim for a $100 million payday, or a $200 million payday—or perhaps it's more than that: they have their heart set on building the next multi-billion dollar, publicly traded company. And so, when they come to a VC to start their next business, they will say, "Hey, I'm a multi-time entrepreneur, I have everyone I need on my team and they'll follow me into this next startup. I would love some inspiration from you, VC." That happens all the time and it's awesome. VCs love investing with a team that's already worked together, a team that is super-hungry has all these great experiences looking to build their next startup. It's such a great working style. It is very possible to invest in an A team which is considering multiple ideas about what business they want to build, especially in the very early days. So now every startup has to change how they organize themselves. They have to reassess their priorities and if they're focused on fundraising, they'll have to rethink growth versus efficient growth. What's most important at the end of the day still comes down to the team because it's possible to build a business in any environment with an amazing team. But the second most important thing is a deep fundamental understanding of the problem. And connected to the validation of the problem is the idea of timing.

FINDING A PROBLEM

When we talk about What, or the problem, it touches a little bit on timing, but you can also look at the problem on a first principles basis, as a standalone concept separate from timing. There are several ways that people land on a problem, one is common and somewhat suboptimal; the other is less common but is a much better approach. One dynamic that happens a lot with founders is that they believe there's a problem, they use logic from their experience to determine that there is a problem, and then, as part of their founder journey, they hear validation that it is a problem. What becomes dangerous for founders in this situation is becoming so focused on a problem that they fall in love with it and they start talking to everybody and anybody about the problem so that they are more or less locked in to that problem, the way they see it. They come to have 100% conviction and when they speak with people they don't know well, those people respond with something like, "Yeah. Cool. Great. I see this problem and it makes sense."

What most people won't do is push back because if a founder is so focused on a problem that they believe exists and needs to be solved, as a non-interested external person it's a little dangerous to tell this founder that you don't think it's a problem. Maybe you'll be concerned that the founder will be upset or react negatively, or maybe you're not vested in the problem so you don't really care. But what happens, unfortunately, is that founders do not get straight talk, they don't get honest feedback about the problem and they end up going down a path that will not be successful. I don't blame the individual for this because not every founder has the access they need to be able to even collect the data, or be exposed to the data they need, to validate that the problem they see is actually a real problem.

For instance, let's say that you have been working in consumer-facing businesses your whole life. You happen to hear news about cybersecurity and you read up on cybersecurity and you think, "You know what? Cybersecurity seems to be the future. I believe this will be a really important problem in the future." You decide to capitalize on that future trend and you want to start building a startup in cybersecurity. Eventually, you land on a problem that people talk about and you think, "I want to solve this problem." Great. But this might be a problem that people have already tried to solve in the past and failed miserably but you wouldn't know that with your lack of understanding about the industry. It feels a lot like the experience of being a student where the professor asks you to do original research because, when that happens, you think, "How could I do any original research in this space? Every problem has already been solved, every question has already been answered." And that's because you've been taught about solved problems by your professors.

The work it takes to think beyond that, to think beyond solved problems and find unsolved problems just requires more time, or it requires more access to data, because at some point when you become a professor, there are too many problems to research. The more you know about an area or space or technology, the more you realize that there are so many problems to be solved. But when you're new to a space you don't see all the problems, you just focus on the one problem you thought of. One common dynamic I've seen over and over again is people chasing a problem that's not meant to be solved, for multiple reasons.

Now, an example of a founder finding a problem successfully, and the ones that I'm most excited about, are the people who obviously have created big businesses. It's easy to pattern match around big businesses and the problem that they solved because hindsight is 20-20, but most people don't see the problem. So the question is, what did these people do differently that allowed them to see a problem with a big market?

One example of a company that solved a problem that was very intuitive but didn't feel intuitive until you were in the market and had firsthand experience with it was a company called ServiceNow. ServiceNow was a software company that required a lot of implementation, development, and configuration services for customers. Because they wanted to be a public company, they wanted to be a software company, not a mix between software and services. And the reason for that is, if you want the highest valuation for your pure software company, you need at least 80% of the revenues to come from software. If you have a hybrid and it's a 50-50 split between software and services, investors will split the company in two and it's actually net negative to the company evaluation. Also, as a pure software company, ServiceNow could focus 100% of their attention on software, and not implementation, service, and coordination.

To stay true to their software vision they created a partner services ecosystem to allow others to implement and service their product. As a result, they were able to grow exponentially because their scale was hundreds of millions based on a cadre of partners. The problem that ServiceNow solved was a problem created by the ecosystem, and they solved it for the ecosystem. They delivered excellent services, they had the trust and credibility of the ecosystem, and they were able to both hire and scale up people to deliver the services through their network of partners. In addition, they could remain focused on software development and could be much more efficient since they didn't need to hire, train, and manage an army of salespeople.

Finding a great problem to solve is a lot more than reading a few articles and coming up with a problem that you see. The best problems are ones where you feel like everything is aligned and all the ingredients are there. The problem is there, it has been validated, and it is a big problem that scales.

4

When = Timing

Timing is a secret weapon in the thought process of the best venture capitalists and founders. It can be applied everywhere, but specifically within venture it is a major factor that can determine whether an investment will be wildly successful or fairly successful or a complete failure. For example, when we talk about the iPod as a successful product, one of the reasons it was possible was because of the timing. The iPod became a reality because we had hard drives that were more resistant, more durable, that we could hold in our hands and shake around without crashing. So the iPod physically and technologically was not possible before a certain period of time, even though the need was always there and the interest was always there.

Another dynamic is also sometimes there's a new problem and a new solution and the interest is there, but the budget is not there. For example, electric cars are a classic example right now and a lot of people are very interested in buying electric cars. The technology has been available for a long time to power cars with electricity, but it was a novelty for most people. We might see one on the road and say to ourselves, "I'm never going to buy that freaking thing, I would never spend $200,000 for a car that can only go a few miles. What would happen if I ever got stranded somewhere?" But then gradually, over time, technology, infrastructure, our trust, the cost, and our budget changed to align to purchasing electric cars and now they're almost the preferred standard in certain geographies. So when we validate a problem, there is a timing element as well.

When people think about the early days of venture, what commonly comes to mind is the tech bubble and all the crazy companies that were funded in the beginning stages of the internet. In those days, in the 1990s, there were a lot of experiments and people mocked a lot of these companies. For example, today we have DoorDash, Instacart, and Uber Eats that are successful and all of them are basically doing what Webvan tried to do 20 years ago—deliver food to customers. Why are these companies successful in the 2020s when Webvan failed in the 1990s? It is because of timing. It never would've worked back then. Whether it is because of the users' comfort in using the Webvan solution or because there wasn't the right technology to support it, the right ingredients weren't there for the Webvan service.

If we compare the timing from the 1990s to today, we can see that we have a completely different set of factors. Today we have mobile phones which are incredibly powerful devices in our hands, and we have easy ubiquitous access to the internet. We have a different way of thinking about labor that was personified by Uber and the Gig economy in the 2020s' generation, for example, where a company doesn't need to have people on their payroll and pay wages and benefits; they can build and depend on a community of independent contractors to deliver the services on their platform. Timing is very different now than it was back then. Actually, one of my longest-term mentors and partner in venture, Alberto, uses a phrase that his father taught him, "Decisions are a snapshot in time." A decision we make today could make a ton of sense but could have made zero sense 10 years ago and it could make zero sense 10 years as well in the future. And so we do need to consider that timing element.

TIMING = ENVIRONMENT

I also refer to "timing" as the environment because it describes all the elements, and building blocks available to a new company. When we think about the environment, we need to think about more than just if it is a good time to start this business. You also must think about who your competitors are and how much funding it may take to capture attention in a market that may already be saturated with well-funded vendors. You need to think about what your customers are feeling or thinking and what their preferences are as well. And you also think about your own self in terms of building your company. For example, what the fundraising environment looks like, or what the hiring environment looks like. And so having a really good sense of our surroundings, of the environment that we're in, really helps to figure out whether an idea that you're chasing or a problem that you want to solve or a solution that you want to build is the right fit for the right environment.

And the key to understanding more deeply the problem and solution you have is understanding that the success of any business is partly driven by timing. And what makes understanding the environment difficult is that environments change and we can't control that component. And if that's true in real life, how do we think about timing in venture capital? Well, that's actually the really fun part of venture because this is what draws us back a little bit to my earlier point about the value of specialization.

SPECIALIZATION LEADS TO SUCCESS, LEADING TO OPTIONALITY

When we look at VCs and their careers, almost every single one of them specialized in an industry in one way, shape, or form. And if we look at people early in their career, while we all start out as generalists, very quickly we are asked to start specializing right after high school in college or in the workforce in some way, shape, or form. It's only when we get into the later stages of our careers—the last half or last quarter—when we are doing so incredibly well that we have all these options and we can go back to becoming a generalist. That's when we can be like Richard Branson, for example, who has a hand in media, healthcare, airline, rail transportation, space, and a number of charitable organizations. When you are successful, you can explore variety and pursue disparate interests because you have options and resources. But in the earlier stages when you don't, when you don't have the wealth that a billionaire might have, it really helps to specialize and find ways to differentiate yourself in this world.

That specialization has a direct impact on your understanding of timing because if you're a specialist, you can understand the environment and see all the different levers and moving pieces. You will see that there is a great problem that is unsolved and is very ripe for disrupting today. You will also see that in some cases there are going to be problems that will never, ever be solved or at least never be solved in our lifetimes. And when you run across those problems, you just let go. It might be painful, it's probably a horrible problem, and we all don't like it, but we can't do anything about it, so we move on. That's where the power of specialization comes in. I specialize in cybersecurity and I understand which conditions are more conducive to building successful cybersecurity startups that reach their market potential. What cybersecurity startups need to thrive differs greatly from consumer companies, or traditional FinTech companies. Every industry has its own dynamic, and, by specializing, those differences will become apparent.

For instance, one great example is Salesforce, which has been the clear leader in customer relationship management (CRM) for more than a decade. How much longer are they going to be a market leader? Probably for a really, really, really long time because that industry is huge and also because of the nature of the CRM space. The cybersecurity industry is very different because we have new threats, we have new technologies, we have new people, and the industry is constantly evolving. The leaders in the industry today cannot stay leaders for a very long time unless they're constantly evolving themselves. And because of that imperative to grow and innovate, there is a lot of opportunity for a startup to become the new leader of a category, or for a startup to create a new category that disrupts an old category and changes the market. There's a lot of innovation and change in cybersecurity that happens in that way.

In the early days of most emerging industries like cybersecurity, growth for most companies came through mergers and acquisitions (M&A) activity because the categories that were being created weren't very large. And with a small category, if you need an exit, the only way to do that is through a merger or acquisition. Now that cybersecurity is more mature—about a $200 billion industry—it's a lot easier to create public companies and in fact we have seen multiple public companies in specific categories. The way to think about the cybersecurity role within an organization is that it takes on every kind of risk related to technology. Lawyers take on every risk related to law, finance takes on every risk related to money, and the security folks take on every risk related to technology. Because technology usage is changing so quickly, the cybersecurity risks change quickly and that leads to innovation, the creation of new categories, and new industry leaders.

But that's just one way of seeing the nuance and it differs for other industries. In a very large consumer industry like advertising (supporting companies like Google, Facebook) or E-commerce (like Amazon) or FinTech (like Square, Stripe), we can see some companies grow virally into what feels like overnight successes because the market size is large and consumer preferences change very quickly.

GENERATIONAL TIMING

In addition to thinking about consumer preferences, technology, and a host of other conditions that impact timing, there is another component of timing that involves generational changes. For instance, if you go back to the Webvan example earlier, we did not have mobile phones or apps, or any way to access the internet other than a computer. That was the primary way of accessing the internet then, but today, we are in a very different world because of mobile phones. And while we can associate mobile phones with the millennial generation, mobile phones are used by people across the world across generations, leading to disruption across many different categories.

E-commerce is now on mobile, but for a long time it was only on the web. At one time no one ever imagined that we would ever do anything else other than buy things on websites. Just like no one thought we would ever do anything else other than buy things in stores. Back when the internet was beginning to grow and become popular, people complained about their experience buying things on the internet because you can't touch, smell, or play with anything. "Why would you ever buy anything on the internet?" People also thought it was very risky to use a credit card on the internet, which also hampered mass adoption. But eventually people became comfortable with new technology and buying things on the internet to the point where now they're willing to buy anything on the internet—even big-ticket items like cars and homes.

These kinds of generational changes reinforce the importance of timing and they can impact everything, not just consumer preferences. Generational changes also move into enterprise preferences. For example, suppose that you're being delighted every day using a really amazing application on your phone as a consumer. You might think, why don't we have this experience at work? Why don't our customers we work with also have this experience? And so what happens is those trends move into enterprise. One fun example is the BlackBerry. For a long time, people used cell phones but Blackberry came out and was able to show people a business-oriented solution just for businesses. Look at how amazing it is. And everyone was thinking, we're going to be using BlackBerries for the rest of our lives. And then people started using the iPhone as consumers and they thought, wait, this is better in some ways, why can't we use the iPhone at work? And eventually the whole enterprise mobile situation changed so that now no one is locked into a specific mobile device at work. You can use Android, you can use Windows phone, you can use iPhone. You can use a BlackBerry, whatever it is. You have lots and lots of options now. That trend was called BYOD (bring your own device) and while it's interesting on its own, it also aligned with software as a service (SaaS) applications. For a long time applications were either installed on your computer or on a server that accessed SaaS applications. Now, most new applications are hosted by "cloud-first" and that'll be remembered as a critical technology trend popularized when the millennial generation became the majority of the workforce.

TIMING AND DISRUPTION

When we think about timing, one way it applies to startups is to think about it as both disrupting existing norms but also as opportunity: what are the things that we can do now that we couldn't do before? And that is where we can leverage the power of technology and, surprisingly, that is also where we can also leverage the value of science fiction. In science fiction we are imagining things that could happen, things that might be possible during the next generation—or even further out. These are things that might never even happen in our lifetimes, that's why it's science fiction. Whereas the opportunity for startups is, especially in the form of technology, that they can make things that should exist within three years, five years, or 10 years of building. And so timing is one factor that is partly intuitive because it comes with life experience, but also partly based on knowledge, because you can learn about timing by reading science fiction or paying attention to what futurists are saying. For most people, including myself, their exposure to timing is in the form of seeing failure and seeing successes and being curious and asking, why was this successful? Why was this a failure?

And if you really want to answer those questions, you'll have to go through every single dimension of the framework I'm sharing. Team—oh, was it the right people involved? What—did they think about the problem deeply and are they solving the right problem? How—did they tackle the market in terms of sales and marketing? We go through all those different questions and eventually, after all that brainstorming, all that introspection, all that questioning and curiosity, that's usually when people land on timing and they're like, "Oh, this solution is before its time." That's a common phrase. "Before its time." But something that I found out while I was learning in venture is that timing is frequently attributed to why a startup failed but not as frequently a reason why they invested. When people talk about venture capital, the standard framework is team, tech, and total addressable market (TAM) and while those are in this framework, timing is frequently omitted.

Timing definitely needs to be considered when it comes to startups, and in investing in general. It's going to be very important for entrepreneurs when they think about what problems they want to solve, because in thinking about timing, they will be able to filter out the problems that they shouldn't solve. An entrepreneur might come up with a great problem that everyone hates, but it's not the right time to solve this problem. And because of that, they can go work on something else instead. Timing is a great way to help people filter out options.

Timing is also something individual investors should think about in their own portfolio, or 401(k), or Roth IRA because it is a great way for people outside of venture and the entrepreneurial ecosystem to think about how timing impacts returns.

For instance, a fun one to think about is the idea that you can't time the public markets, and so you'll often hear the advice that you shouldn't do day trading, or don't try to predict when the market is going to go up and down. It's really impossible to time the market because no matter how much data you have, it's impossible to predict the future. But there's a good version of timing in the public markets and that is the advice to buy low and sell high. You can't buy the very bottom of the market, but it's very clearly better timing to buy when the market is low-ish and it's very good timing to sell when the market is high-ish. Rather than time the market or randomly buy or sell, some recognition of timing will lead to better returns. Timing is a factor in all our lives.

Another way of thinking about timing is in the form of our personal careers. Early in your career you have very few skills, you're hungry, you want to work hard, you have great grades to show that you are very smart and very hard-working, but you also need to think about what job you can go after. You may want to be a CEO of a global corporation but today you don't have the resources nor the experience to be a CEO of a large multinational company. Your ambitions are before your time.

Another component that's important to think about where timing plays a role, is in choosing an industry. For instance, the growth of electric cars is very high and a person could say, "Eureka! One day electric cars are going to be the standard, so I should find a job in that industry." So good timing is not choosing to go into the traditional car industry, for instance, especially if you believe that electric cars are the future or, more specifically, not going into the gasoline engine building industry, because those cars will inherently be disrupted by electric cars. There is a timing element to career choice and thinking about timing is a way to invest in your own career, to make sure that you start building your own career with a great future path available for you.

THE RISE AND FALL OF COMPANIES

One area where it is critical to think about timing is by looking at leading companies. One thing I do in my role as a venture capitalist is look at leading companies and it's clear that they constantly rise and fall. If you look at the top 10 companies today, and you think about the top 10 companies a decade ago or two decades ago, the list keeps changing— they are not the same companies. It's very difficult to stay a top-10 company for a long time and what that means as an entrepreneur is that you can pick a leader and try to compete against it. And that's where the importance of timing comes into play. If you try to compete against a leader when they are rising, when everyone loves them, when everyone's excited by them because they have a cool product and everyone's using it during the first couple of years, you will probably lose. For example, when people buy their first iPhone they're like, "Oh, my gosh, this is brilliant. This is genius. This is the best freaking thing ever." But now, years later, we're in a time where the iPhone is still awesome, but we're not so delighted by it anymore. There are no more surprises. Oh, it's a little faster. Oh, the camera's a little better, but, hey, where's the new design? If you wanted to compete against Apple 10 years ago as a startup, my advice would be, don't compete against a leader when it is rising because it is very difficult to topple a leader in their prime. Try to compete against a leader when it's falling, when it's no longer as interesting, when it's losing its novelty or luster.

It is so incredibly difficult for a leader to stay the leader, even for a category that they've created. So Facebook was not the very first social media company out there but they became the leader and they basically defined what's possible in social media. And while Facebook helped create this category of social media, it's very, very hard to preserve that lead. Facebook is on their downward trajectory and the questions are, will they be able to recover or will they be like many other companies that go on their downward trajectory and eventually get acquired by another company, get rolled in, or get acquired by private equity, where they will find financial engineering applied to it? I don't know, but when you think about the timing dimension, you can see that Facebook was rising when they bought Instagram. Instagram was a startup that was able to find a niche where Facebook wasn't doing well and Instagram competed with Facebook and eventually got acquired by Facebook. And now Instagram is one of the crown jewels in the Facebook portfolio. The timing dimensions are telling and as a VC, LP, or entrepreneur, it is best to be super-mindful of the trajectory of a leader. That doesn't mean that you just give up and stop trying to compete. It means that you should find something that you can do exceptionally well versus going straight head-to-head in competition with a dominant company like Facebook, for example. Acquiring emerging companies through M&A is another way to stay competitive and relevant.

And so what was Instagram's difference? What is it that threatened Facebook enough that Facebook acquired them? Well, photo-based social media, right? The way it approached it with filters and other features was very different from what Facebook was doing. In fact, when Facebook acquired Instagram for a billion dollars, it wasn't an obvious purchase—in hindsight, it now seems like they should have acquired them sooner, but back then it was not so obvious. Timing is one of the things to be super-mindful of, especially in the form of the environment that you're in. You need to be very cognizant of who your competitors are, what your customers' preferences are, what technology can enable. You need to know how budgets are moving around and changing both consumer decisions and enterprise decisions. Because once you understand that, then you can choose your path through this environment and that can be your path to success. But if you do want to become a huge business, go find a leader that is not doing well, that's on their downward trajectory because that is when they are vulnerable to being disrupted.

A downward trajectory is one factor, but there is a second factor connected to it and that is: what do customers feel about the company and product? It's not the case that if a company is on a downward trajectory that customers will stop using it. Some customers are fine staying with a company on a downward trajectory. It might not be exciting but it's fine. It's a solution. So in understanding timing, it's not enough to understand the trajectory, what you need to find is a company where the downward direction of the leader is impacting the customers' priorities, the leader's solution is now causing them pain. And that's when it's a good opportunity to try to disrupt it. And you see this over and over again.

One great example of a company that has recovered and has maintained their leadership position is Microsoft. There was a time when it was not great being an employee at Microsoft, and it was not an exciting company. But since about 2017 or so, Microsoft has become an exciting company again, especially within the enterprise side of their business. And what did Microsoft do to recover? They basically abandoned their strategy of putting Windows everywhere and instead decided to put Microsoft software everywhere and then they invested in Azure, they improved Office 365, they improved Windows—none of these were mind-blowing new developments. But the way that they did it was based on strategy, based on recognizing their leadership position already and then providing additional features to their current customers for free, more or less, to start delighting them again. Their approach was, "Hey, we're the leader and if you continue sticking with us, you don't have to go look for other solutions to these problems. We have taken care of them for you."

5

Where = Market

"Where," or market, is one of the key variables that VCs look at but it's helpful to think about market in terms of what kind of investor you are. At a high level, "where" is referring to the total addressable market (TAM) of what this startup is going after. The term "total addressable market" is a concept or an estimate like, "Hey, how many ping pong balls can fit into an airplane? Hey, how many cars are on the road in the United States?" And to answer those questions, you do a lot of math basically to figure out, okay, this is how many ping pong balls will fit on an airplane, or how many potential cars there are on the road.

Those examples might seem trivial but the reason why TAM is important is because it gives you a sense of opportunity, it gives you some thinking around how large the world is and how much of the market you have to own or contribute to become a very successful business. If a market seems small, do you have to become the "big fish in a small pond" to reach a certain level of success? If the market is large and crowded, how much white space is there really for a startup to grow?

The second high-level thought process to add when it comes to TAM or market size, is there's also a widely held belief that the winner of a market generally owns the vast majority of that market as well. And when you think about things like search engines, for example, we always think of Google or when you think of facial tissues, we generally think of Kleenex. These companies are the clear leaders and because of that, they generally own the market's mindshare.

One of the biggest reasons a company owns the market is because most people don't have the time to do diligence on all 20 options, so when there's a leader, it usually makes people's decisions a lot easier. With a clear leader, people know what is "best" and then they can more easily choose between "best" and something that is slightly different, based on their own preferences. Maybe it's cost or maybe the company understands them better, or maybe there's something unique to them or their company. One example of preferring something else is WhatsApp. Within the US, there were already a lot of messaging systems and SMS was the clear leader but, internationally, SMS didn't work very well across different countries. And the cost for SMS internationally was very high. What WhatsApp did was provide an alternative to the best, and over time they became the best for their specific niche and the international market is way bigger than the domestic market.

HOW VCs LOOK AT TAM

When it comes to the market that you're in, a lot of people start with TAM, and then once they have a reasonable guess of that, they can understand how big a business you can build within this market. TAM is one of the classic factors that people consider when they say, for instance, "team, tech, and TAM," but there are nuances to TAM that are useful to understand. TAM actually is interpreted differently based on different VC firms. Some VC firms have this perspective of, "Hey, we only invest in companies that can go public and if a company wants to go public, they must be targeting a big TAM, and they have to also become one of the leaders of that TAM." Because of that investment style or goal, these VCs don't invest in companies that are serving a niche—they won't invest if something doesn't fit with their investment goals. If a company only has a potential of becoming a $50 million/year or $100 million/year revenue business, they're not excited, they're not interested, and they'll only invest in the company if they can see that company one day generating a billion dollars of revenue or multiple billion dollars of revenue. When we think about those types of companies that can grow to the billions, we're thinking of Apple, Google, Facebook, and others that are household names.

But there are other VC firms that are comfortable investing in companies that only generate $100 million or $200 million in revenue/year because those companies can become really great acquisition targets for private equity firms. If the revenue is very sticky and consistent, if it's very predictable, and if it's a high profit margin business, private equity could eventually acquire this business and add it to other sticky high-profit companies and create some nice outcomes as well. The big reality is that often, when people invest in a market, they don't really know how big that market will get.

For instance, DoorDash is a good company to illustrate a way to think about TAM. With DoorDash as a potential company to invest in, we'd start thinking about how much delivery of food happens on a global basis. That's a very large number and so that TAM is large. But the second question is, how many people will buy food from an app that's delivered via an app? That question was completely unanswerable when DoorDash and Uber Eats and all these other companies started. That's where the bet is.

On the one hand, there is TAM but, on the other, there is SAM, which is the serviceable addressable market—the market size of the people who can actually use the service or product based on your business model. Finally, there is serviceable obtainable market (SOM) which is the percentage of SAM that you can realistically acquire. Where do we go from here?

There are really two lines of thinking in VC. One is to think about startups that can become public businesses, and the other is to think about companies who will likely become revenue accelerant as part of a large business (could be public or not). Because large public businesses require hundreds of millions of revenue, each specialization typically can only sustain a couple of new leaders per year. And what that means is when you are a VC firm that only invests in leaders of big categories, you cannot become a niche specialist because you have to be able to invest across all of infrastructure, for example. And even then, that might be too much of a limitation. That's why a lot of times you'll see firms invest both across consumer and enterprise generally because they are looking for companies that have the ability to "return a fund" in a large TAM.

The other dynamic that you think about when you're an investor in this bucket is that a lot of these VCs also generally have large funds, billion dollar plus in some cases. And when you think about the business model as a VC firm, your goal is to return at least 2x to that fund at the very minimum but realistically targeting over 3x for a good outcome and then over 5x if you are looking to be one of the top funds. If you are a $1 billion plus fund, how are you going to return $5 billion back to your investors? You can only invest in companies that will return billions of dollars in value. And the only companies that can do that are the ones with a very large TAM. The appropriate VC learning to bring up here is called "the power law." A small percentage of investments typically yield the majority of a VC fund's returns.

What happens in the VC industry is that if you find firms in this category, they are very limited in terms of how much specialization they can do, on one hand. And then, on the other hand, these very large multi-stage VC firms also make a lot of investments in companies that could become a large TAM or are targeting a large TAM, but ultimately the category they're in doesn't become a large category. Even if they sell the company for a billion dollars—which seems like a rare amount—there are VC firms that could still consider that a failure, because if the returns back to their fund are only $100 million or maybe $200 million, that's not enough to drive a billion-dollar fund to a 2x return at the minimum. That's one school of thought, typically pursued by multi-stage VC firms, where they are generally looking for the biggest winners or generally looking for companies that can generate more than a billion of revenue and that can one day be worth more than $10 billion valuation.

The other school of thought is more commonly found in specialist funds and funds that are less than a billion dollars. Unlike the multi-stage firms, specialized firms don't have the issue of selling a company for a billion dollars and regretting it. Because, if you are a $300 million or $400 million fund and you sell a business for a billion dollars, your return is $100 or $200 million and that is a pretty big dent in your goal of achieving a 3x to 5x return. A smaller VC firm has the option to pursue a strategy to invest in companies that are likely to be acquired, or likely to have a smaller IPO. The key difference is that while you do need a large TAM, it doesn't have to be the largest of the largest, and the company you invest in doesn't have to be the clear leader in the category. That gives you the opportunity to target more categories, help build more categories, and have a realistic outcome via a sub-$500 million merger or acquisition, for example. For a smaller VC firm, the differentiation is being able to get a lot of volume of $500 million to one billion dollar acquisitions because if you can do several of these, that will be more than enough to generate a 3x–5x fund, especially when you consider the collective value of the remaining other companies in the fund. The economics are very different and that's why you usually see specialist funds or early-stage funds being less than a billion dollars.

Lastly, there is also the early-stage-only strategy of investment which involves working with companies in their most riskiest and uncertain stages at lower valuations. Typically, in this stage, VCs are very hands on as well and collectively the lower valuation and additional time required ensure early-stage VCs more ownership in these companies. With the large starting ownership figures in these companies, it's common for an early-stage fund to be returned its capital multiple times over from just one exit.

Remember, a fund will typically invest in 15–20 companies and to use a baseball metaphor, if you hit a lot of singles and you have a smaller fund, you can still return the 3x–5x that you're aiming to return. And if you strike out, it's going to be a lot less consequential. With a smaller fund, you also can't immediately concentrate all of your funds in specific companies either, because if those few miss, then it really hurts your ability to make multiple returns on that fund. That is why typically funds will have limits on the maximum percentage of the fund that you can invest into one specific company. For the multi-stage funds, they have the luxury of investing larger checks as well, when it is a small percentage of their fund. The dynamic is, if you're a smaller fund and you're a specialist, that allows you to balance the risk where you can aim to hit lots and lots of singles and maybe—maybe—get lucky and you get a home run.

But if you are a very large fund, you have to hit multiple home runs in order to win because those singles don't make a dent in the fund.

STRATEGY FOR VCs BASED ON THE SIZE OF THE FIRM

Regardless of whether you're an entrepreneur, investor, or a Next-Gen VC working at a venture capital firm, the way that you add value for yourself or for your firm differs, based on the strategy and the size of your VC fund. Larger funds typically can hire more resources and smaller funds typically have to find ways to focus.

For example, if we look at the specialist fund, which is more typical across early-stage investment funds, these funds have the ability to provide breadth in their specialist niche. Or if this isn't a specialist fund, perhaps the fund can focus on investing in the best companies based in New Orleans, for example.

This is a lot like the classic tradeoffs we sometimes have to make when working with services-oriented organizations like real estate, for instance. Sometimes you have a home that only someone local could understand how to sell and sometimes you have a destination home better suited for a large established broker with connections across the world.

In many ways, the smaller firms also win over entrepreneurs with hands-on value-add, like, "We're a smaller fund and we can give you more attention, we can give you more focus. We have more focused resources dedicated to your specific problem." If you are working with or at a multi-stage mega fund, your strategy is inherently different since there are only so many fund-returning businesses out there, and only a limited set of companies that will one day dominate a category. In a mega fund you need to have great coverage of the highest potential businesses bar none. Even better to have the coverage to invest in early when it is more realistic to acquire a larger percentage ownership. To do that, it also requires, surprise, surprise, specialization!

Because there are also many other mega funds, large firms will typically also create a team of specialists within the firm itself. Extending the real estate strategy, if they wanted to provide the best of both the local firm and the global firm, they also need a local office in the geographies they want to participate in. When they do that, they can then provide both the value of the specialization in the space and the resources a large firm can inherently provide with economies of scale. With this multi-pronged strategy, multi-stage funds can play a different game than the smaller firms, making many smaller firms jealous!

Now when it comes to the economics as an entrepreneur, if given the option of more capital at better valuations, generally most people prefer trading less company ownership, especially if the company is a huge success. This, however, isn't the only factor that matters when it comes to choosing which VC firm you are working with. Another important factor is the board member, you should ask, who will be in the trenches with you?

In many ways, we can continue to compare VC firms to professional services organizations like accounting, consulting, investing, and real estate. In some services organizations you get to work directly with a partner and the partner doesn't have a large team. While the partner is experienced, they can't cover very many clients. And because they can't cover very many clients, there is a natural difference in the amount of attention that you get from them. There are other services organizations that have large teams of people so they can manage a lot of clients, but you as a client sometimes do not get very much time with the most senior person on that team. For instance, continuing the real estate comparison, many times the most successful brokers have large teams and can get access to bigger houses, higher prices. The flip side though? The sellers have also to get comfortable working with the up-and-coming members of the team or keep fighting for the name-brand brokers' attention, especially if you are on the smaller end. This is also true at investment banking firms. Each firm has a sweet spot valuation that they plan to transact in. If you are on the low end of that range or even below that range, be prepared to leverage the brand name firm's resources but primarily you will have the attention of the more junior bankers.

CALCULATING TAM AND WHAT DOES IT IMPLY?

This has been a question I've been asking myself and looking at VCs for data points for years. Is there a standard calculation? So far the furthest hypothesis I've gotten is that the vast majority probably trust analyst firms like Gartner. What is more important to note here is that, despite there not being a standard way of calculating TAM, this is still one of the most commonly considered decision-making criteria in VC: "team, tech and TAM."

My next question was, "OK, what is a large enough TAM?" and that has been a fun exercise over time in asking questions like . . . How big a TAM is required for there to be one IPO-sized company or multiple? Is TAM a zero-sum game? For one category to rise, does it require another adjacent category to fall? Is there a timing component to TAM? Is it organically created or is it catalyzed by startups/innovation? And, again, I would say that this is where specialization will help you answer these questions because they are different per industry.

In my specialization, I measure TAM in orders of 10. Is the total budget for this category in the 10s of millions of dollars, 100s of millions or billions of dollars? If the TAM is less than $100 million, the most likely investment in that category is an early-stage company that is building a category that could grow exponentially. So we have to believe in both that company and that category. If the TAM is in the 100s of millions of dollars, there are already multiple companies in the space. How are they individually doing and is there room for a startup to grow in that space? Is there a possibility that this TAM could grow some more? Lastly, if the TAM is in the billions, then there are likely already multiple companies in the category, each with great strengths. Is there room for growth or, if needed, disruption in the space? If the company is meant for M&A, is there room to participate to get to a stage where an acquirer would benefit from the company and their solution being a part of their portfolio?

6

Why = Solution

When I was first creating this framework, I initially called this component of the framework "customer empathy." My rationale was that when you look at companies in the long term, including companies that can sustain their success for a long time, one reason for their prolonged performance is that these companies have been able to serve their customers—existing and new—and in multiple different ways. One example, on the consumer side, is Apple. They have been able to serve the consumer in multiple different ways, really incredibly well. Starting with the Mac and continuing with the iPhone, iPod, iPad, Apple Music, they really built an ecosystem around their company. They've continued building so many tools and solutions that have delighted their consumers over and over again and they have been able to serve both consumers and enterprise with their products. But the key thing here is, what are they really good at? They're really good at serving their consumers, the tech consumers, with products that keep those same customers coming back again and again. Apple didn't create completely new products for completely new customers, but products that evolve with the same customers.

Another really good example on the enterprise side is Microsoft. Microsoft has demonstrated over and over again their ability to serve the enterprise. Starting from, of course, Windows, the operating system, but then also the Office suite of applications, and then one wild card for them, serving a different type of customer has been gaming, with Xbox. But you still look at Microsoft's overall business and if you ask, "Why are they successful?," it is because of their ability to serve the enterprise customer and develop a suite of productivity solutions that allow those customers to use technology to create solutions, create value, and create outputs.

Microsoft and Apple are good examples of companies that served their customers with new products to delight them, but there are other companies that serve differentiated customers, like Amazon or the companies that make up the holdings of Elon Musk. Amazon is an example of a company that built a really big enterprise business with Amazon Web Services (AWS), as well as all the retail sales on the consumer side. And Elon Musk is providing products and services to very different customers with Tesla, Solar City, Starlink, SpaceX, and now, Twitter. He has prioritized a lot of different users, a lot of different consumers with his businesses. And although it's too early to say whether he'll be able to pull it off, it's a good example of someone creating businesses with multiple different users.

Of course, there is a long list of companies that lost their way and became one-hit wonders that didn't survive. Blockbuster, for instance, was a company that served the consumer incredibly well, especially by providing them media entertainment. But as technology quickly enabled different experiences and consumers' needs changed, unfortunately Blockbuster did not evolve very well, they didn't see streaming like Netflix did. And, as a result, they eventually went out of business, while Netflix right now has evolved from DVD mail rental, to streaming, to content creator, and now is experimenting with gaming. But all of Netflix's changes are still around the same similar idea of entertaining consumers.

SOLVING ONE PROBLEM REALLY WELL

The examples of Apple, Microsoft, and Amazon and all these long-time successful companies stem from their customer empathy, but I think the very first bar, the most difficult one, is just starting with serving one customer profile incredibly well. Instead of serving multiple customers or, more importantly, building multiple platforms that solve your customers' problems, it's important to solve one problem for one customer profile. When we think about the vast majority of companies, the vast majority are not Amazon, Tesla, Microsoft, or Netflix. Most companies become a real business by first solving one problem really well.

You might have aspirations to become a global powerhouse, but you can actually do that by solving one problem very well, because first you might be surprised by how big the TAM becomes. And if it's a huge TAM, solving that one problem could lead to a gigantic business. For example, one large TAM that many people have exposure to is real estate. Realtors are solving one problem and you usually see a realtor doing either residential real estate or commercial real estate, but not both. You usually see them only doing one, and, even then, they sometimes only serve certain types of clientele or certain types of properties, or certain locations. And if you're good at real estate, you can make enormous sums of money, you can grow a very large company—because you are solving one problem in a large TAM.

What's most important is having a really deep understanding of the solution that you are creating for the problem, which is the "What" in the framework. When you think about the solution, the solution is not always very easy, and not always very obvious. I mentioned earlier the example of the iPhone and today it seems obvious as a solution to communicating, and we cannot imagine a world without smartphones. But creating that solution is monumentally difficult because there is a lot of leeway in determining what the right solution is for an important problem. In Chapter 3, the "What" chapter, I talked about how important it is to deeply understand the problem and here in the "Why" chapter I'll talk about the solution and why it is difficult to create a solution.

One of the things that happens over and over again with VCs is that we have a lot of people come in and say, "Hey, this is a real problem," and they can demonstrate that they understand the problem really well. But unfortunately, the act of creating the why—the solutions—is incredibly difficult because there is so much leeway, there are so many different ways of thinking about a solution. We can go back to the horse versus car example, which was a solution to transportation that seems like a no-brainer now, but when you asked people back in the days with the horses what would be a solution, it was a faster horse. The solution was not obviously a car, but now it is obviously the car and who knows what the future will look like. And so that is the depth of understanding around the solution that you need and it's really critical to understand the solution well because there are so many nuances and creativity required when you think about a solution that has never existed before. A successful company is built on a solution that takes into account deep customer empathy and solves those problems in a way that the customer would want it to be solved, or solves it in a way the customer didn't even realize was possible for it to be solved. But once a customer sees a solution, they cannot not see it. They cannot imagine the world without that solution.

One of the classic failure patterns that we see a lot in VC is a solution in search of a problem. That is a phrase we hear a lot in VC for why companies fail. It is so common for someone to build a solution without understanding the customer deeply. When you build a solution without applying all those important nuances and then say, "Hey, this solution is the salvation for this problem," you're likely to hear from a potential customer, "No, I don't agree with you at all," or "Interesting solution. Let me get back to you if I'm interested in the future."

BUILDING THE RIGHT SOLUTION

This is where the importance of team construction comes into play because you cannot go into solving a problem and building a solution without flexibility and openness. It's also where a design partner can help. A design partner can help a company go from, "Hey, there are millions of ways I can solve this problem" to "This is one way we would love to see the problem solved." A design partner can help the startup start crystalizing the important factors and help minimize the myriad of options to the one path that they should take. For instance, a customer might say, "Hey, something that's really important to me is cost. It cannot cost more than $X because I cannot spend more than $X for it." And that actually takes out a lot of solutions because some solutions are very expensive to run, and as a result, the business can never get off the ground.

Another common customer response might be, "Hey, I only have three people on my team and this solution cannot take more than half of one of my employees' time to manage." That feedback will force you to minimize the number of solutions that you can create because you cannot create something that will require one person to manage it full-time. Another customer might say, "Hey, I can only purchase this solution digitally." That, again, changes all the different ways you can provide a solution for a customer because now the in-person dynamics of someone first experiencing something are absent. So the "solution" involves a lot of nuance and it is equally as difficult as figuring out the problem you want to solve because of the complexity of details that come into play.

It's much more common to build a solution after you understand the customer really well, and I would argue that some of the biggest innovations in our lives weren't solutions in search of problems. The most successful businesses do not have a "build it and they will come" mentality and even those innovations that seem that way, like the iPhone, weren't created by an inventor and then put out into the world. The iPhone was successful because somebody deeply understood the problem, somebody deeply understood the users, and they experimented and tinkered and then eventually built a conviction and the data that validated that the iPhone needed to exist. And then, once they got that validation, that's when they built the confidence to bet the company on the iPhone and cannibalize their iPod business with the iPhone.

There are instances where a solution exists and it does get matched with a problem. For example, 3M's Post-It notes come to mind. Several scientists in the 3M lab invented a glue that they thought was novel but they couldn't get anyone at 3M interested in the product, so they applied it to small note paper and went to the CEO of 3M and asked him to share it with people. The CEO took the product to the Board meeting and several days later got calls from the

Board members for more "sticky notes" because their executive assistants loved them. That's an example of a solution in search of a problem that actually worked, but it is very rare. The best solutions are very purposeful and they are based on data and a deep understanding of customers. A product like the iPhone wouldn't exist if Apple did not have a deep understanding of both the problem and the user, and then package it all up into the beautiful solution that the iPhone was.

The customer is involved in two of these six factors or pillars of Who, What, When, Where, Why, and How—they are involved in the problem (the "What") and they're involved in the solution (the "Why"). We've all heard the phrase that the customer is royalty and in many cases that's true because if we didn't have customers and we didn't have revenue, we wouldn't have businesses.

Customers are the lifeblood of the company in two important ways: we have to divide the customers' demands in terms of the problems that they have, and that's the "What" in this framework. And then we have to deeply understand the solutions from the customers' perspective, and that's the "Why" in the framework. The companies that do those two things well, that match the right problem to the right solution in a large market become the successful public companies.

It's the second iteration that is always the most troubling and that's when the company needs to go back to their roots. They need to go back to understanding yet again the problem that they want to solve, they need to create the right solution, and they need to understand who the customer they're serving is. And if you can't go back to your roots and start all over again—which is a ton of work—you'll be punished in the market. One example of a company where we still do not have the answers and we don't know how successful they will be is Meta, Facebook's gigantic investment of billions of dollars into the metaverse world. And the main issue with Meta, in my opinion, is, who is the customer? What is the problem? We know the solution, we know that there's this concept of a metaverse and you have an avatar in this digital world, but what is the problem? The problem Meta is solving is so unclear, who the customer is for Meta is also so unclear. And that's why the public markets are penalizing Meta for spending all that money because they haven't made it very clear to us, the public, what problem they're solving and which customer they are solving it for. They're just showing us the solution.

BUILDING A SUSTAINABLE BUSINESS

There are so many one-hit wonders, which is fine if you're serving a large TAM, or you've created a whole new category, but the problem all companies face sooner or later is creating a sustainable business. By sustainable business, I mean a business where you've created a solution to a problem at the right price—the price that allows you to be profitable enough to sustain the company. And one of the questions VCs ask is, is this a sustainable business? Is this a real business? Or is this a scenario where a second round of capital won't be possible to raise because they cannot sustain the business standalone, nor grow enough to attract follow-on capital? Building a company, especially one that isn't profitable and depends on VC funding to continue operating, can certainly resemble a tightrope.

7

How = Scale

I've spent a lot of time thinking about how to align my learning to the "How," and in my earliest days I thought this factor only referred to go-to-market execution, especially when we started to see the growth investors layer in KPIs that were predominantly sales-centric. Over time, though, directing my attention to companies with 100 or more employees, I started realizing that companies scaled not because of just revenue but overall, and that includes people.

When we evaluate a team in the "Who" part of the framework, we're asking questions directly related to leadership. As investors we obviously get visibility into leadership but we don't get visibility of the team underneath the leadership, and we need some way to assess the team underneath the leadership. We need to understand the scale of the machine being built by the leadership if we want to make good decisions. So, because the "How" is all about execution, and execution is all about people, there is some overlap between the "Who"—which is the leadership team, and the "How"—which is how the overall company grows to meet market demand.

What's most important about the "How" in VC thought is that we can't do an extensive audit of an organization when evaluating a company for scale. Typically a company that has already started to scale and has validation that it can continue to scale is a more mature startup. In these scenarios, it is not uncommon for numbers to speak more clearly than any number of interviews could provide.

When it is possible to summarize indicators of scalability, efficiency, and success in KPIs, that is, when the act of performing due diligence on a startup can scale itself. Start with the easiest and most objective way of measuring success in the business setting: revenue. At the highest level, if you're spending to generate revenue, you have a machine. If you're spending less capital than it takes to provide the solution, then you have built a profitable machine. It's sort of like the fable of the golden goose—if you can put $1 into a machine and get $3 out, you can do that every single day forever. How you build that machine is the essence of building a company.

Compensation and Output

There is no "right" answer on compensation because everyone is going to come into the organization with different personal needs. Maybe they have family needs with a sick parent or lots of kids at home, or maybe they are a single parent. Maybe they are at the point where their life is very scrappy and they're eating ramen noodles and couch surfing. Maybe they want to be traveling the world and working from Thailand on the beach instead of in San Francisco in a very expensive apartment. There are all sorts of different personal needs that people have.

When I think about the dynamic of personal needs and the organization, it really comes down to output. As long as the output is there and the price it costs to create the output makes sense, then who cares where a person is coming from? Who cares what their personal dynamic is?

Unfortunately, there are going to be some instances where someone just cannot work, not because of a physical disability, but because some really important life event happened. Maybe it's a death in the family or an intense divorce or breakup—anything that might impact someone. I have founders who have, within their family, experienced all kinds of crazy things—suicides of loved ones, drug dependencies, accidents. There are all kinds of different dynamics that we can't control. That's just life. What it really comes down to is output, because in a startup, there's just no room for inefficiency.

THE SALES ORGANIZATION

There's one phrase I like from Dave DeWalt, a CEO and board member on multiple public companies, that sums up the importance of the sales organization, "Technology is a game of inches, but sales is a game of miles." That emphasizes the point that if you have an organization that knows how to sell and market, you can out-compete every other company, every single day. That is completely true in the startup world, especially in enterprise technology and certain consumer products. One reason why that happens is that there are customers who know they are buying inferior technology, but they're buying it from a better company. Why is it a better company? There might be many reasons, but one big reason is that customers want to buy a product from a company that will be around for 5 or 10 years and will continue developing their product. And the best companies will continue to develop their products and also get better as an organization—they will continue to become more efficient and increase their ROI, which gives them staying power. They'll be able to make acquisitions so that they can expand their product lines.

Some companies with phenomenal technology might be a one-hit wonder. They might not raise any more money, they might go out of business in the next six months. So it's risky to purely purchase something for technology reasons and just because it's great technology right now doesn't mean it's going to be good technology in the future. And it doesn't mean that a company is also a good company that will be around for a long time as well.

So, as a result, sales and marketing actually become one of the most important factors in a company's success. This factor is traditionally more of a later-stage venture capital evaluation criterion, because in the very early stages when a company is a seed-stage company and they have three people, you really can't be evaluating them on the sales organization that they're going to build. But it is still one of those things that makes or breaks an organization because if you do not have a phenomenal sales and go-to-market organization, you cannot become a public company. There is just no possibility.

So we're faced with a dilemma: If an early-stage company is too early to build a sales organization, how do you evaluate whether they can ever build one? It sounds impossible but it's not. The easiest way, and where almost everyone starts, is by analyzing the numbers and by looking at the metrics. For example, one metric is sales cycle: How long does it take to sell to a customer? Does it take them a year? Does it take them two years? If it takes that long, that raises a lot of uncertainty, because if you meet a customer and you think, "Oh, my gosh, a year from now, two years from now, they're going to buy," how do you prioritize this customer now? How do you know that this is the one customer that you should be spending all your time with?

Time is a scarce resource when it comes to a startup. If you have a company with a sales cycle of three months, then that's a huge benefit because you do the work, you get the results, you get the data, the feedback loops come back really, really quickly, and then you have insight.

Another metric that tells a lot about a company's sales is the annual recurring revenue (ARR) per employee, the amount of recurring revenue that a customer pays a vendor every year. When we think about employee compensation, we also think about that as a yearly metric so ARR per employee gives you a sense of how much revenue this company is making per employee. Is the revenue that's being generated sustaining the costs of each employee? For example, if you have a company that's at $10,000 ARR per employee and the compensation across the workforce is $150,000 per employee, then you can see right there that company is really inefficient and it's going to take a really long time for that company to go from $10,000 ARR per employee to $300,000 ARR per employee.

Sales cycle and ARR are some of the high-level metrics that people look at and another very common one is the Rule of 40. That's something that we apply in the public markets as well but basically the Rule of 40 is figuring out both (1) the profitability of a company, and (2) how fast it is growing. If you add those two numbers up and if it's over 40, then it might be a good investment. It doesn't matter which of those two variables are driving the metric above 40, it could be either profit or growth.

For example, let's say a company has zero growth every single year—they are stagnant in growth but they're generating 50% profitability every single year. Phenomenal. You have a company that is doing incredibly well. And it works the other way, too. Suppose that a company is generating zero profit every year but is doubling every year in growth—that's 100%, which is really great and is way over the Rule of 40. The initial stages of determining whether or not a go-to-market machine works is by analyzing some of these easy-to-access metrics like sales cycle, ARR, profitability, and growth.

SALES ORGANIZATION AND CUSTOMER ALIGNMENT

The second component of determining whether a go-to-market (GTM) machine works is by looking at the sales and marketing functions at an organization and asking yourself:

- Do the departments align? Are they working well together?
- Do they have a good understanding of their ideal customer profile (ICP), their target customers by segment, geography, use case, and buying situation?
- Did they structure and tool their GTM accordingly, accommodating the customer journey along the way, from awareness to consideration to evaluation, conversion, retention, and advocacy?

For example, if a startup is targeting Fortune 1000 companies, then typically it should have a direct sales model there because each of those customers is used to being wined and dined. They're used to having a dedicated account executive, for example, with a clear account strategy and roadmap that will often include a sales engineer to help them implement the product and understand how it will be used within their organization. So, if you're selling to Fortune 1000 customers with tens of thousands of employees, that requires a lot of people and a lot of expenses and those customers should be spending more than a middle-market customer with, say, 500 employees. A middle-market customer doesn't want attention, doesn't want to talk to salespeople—they hate talking to salespeople—and they just want to buy with a credit card and move on. They probably don't have a lot of crazy custom unique things and they probably are very similar to, and recognize that they're similar to, other companies around their same size. Middle-market customers are thinking purely about the form of efficiency: "How much does this thing cost? What is the cheapest way to solve my problem?"

In either case, marketing and business development representatives (BDRs) play a key role at the top of the funnel, optimizing the product messaging and positioning (especially against competition), and enabling startup teams to test which tactics will work most effectively.

The sales cycles for middle-market customers are usually shorter and you can't have a dedicated account executive just for that company so you have to have a different model. You probably should have a Business Development Representative (BDR) using a tool like Salesforce, where they go out, generate the leads by calling and reaching out, often based on digital marketing campaign, and then help close those customers. And, finally, if you have customers who are spending anywhere from a few dollars to 10,000 dollars, then your sales organization has to be about transactions because everything will be based on credit cards. For example, Zoom is a company that started out not needing a sales organization because early versions of their platform were self-service. If a customer wanted Zoom, they could use their own credit card, buy it, and move on. It was low-touch/no-touch, requiring little-to-no customer service or selling, enabling smaller transactions at scale. Today, Zoom has greatly developed its platform. It's easy-to-use product and freemium model (anyone can create an account and have calls of 40 minutes or less) drove so much user affinity, that it spread quickly throughout different communities and organizations who then converted to enterprise for more advanced, team-based functionality.

Whether the sales machine that a company built is aligned to customer needs is a key factor to evaluate over time, and everyone will have a different opinion. Some people will think this is the perfect sales machine at this point in time while other people will think this is the worst sales machine and it is not the right fit at this point in time. Another dynamic you would look at is how leads are generated—who is generating the opportunities that are moving through the sales funnel? There are many, many books written about sales and how to build a sales machine, and it's possible to dive deep into any of these topics. But with a limited amount of time to make a decision, the metrics I've outlined above are probably going to be all the data you'll have to understand the sales organization. It may come down to a gut feeling, especially if you are investing in a very early-stage company and the important things are the metrics and your answers to the questions: is the sales organization designed well? Is it functioning well? Is the team curious, learning, and growing? Is there an opportunity to refine it in a productive way?

THE TECHNOLOGY ORGANIZATION

Technology differs from both sales and go-to marketing because technology is something where you think about it in terms of group dynamics, not so much on the actual technology. Sales and marketing are like a coin-operated machine where you put in money and you get money back and the question is, does the money you pay in pay for what you're doing? Technology, which I define as both product and engineering, is a lot more subjective to determine whether or not a product organization is working well. Instead of measuring key performance indicators (KPIs) to measure a product organization, the best thing I've learned with the product organization is hire great leaders. Hire leaders who have built commercial solutions before, solutions that have had a lot of customers throw rocks at them before, because what a leader with that experience can do, is they can prevent those rocks from happening the next time around and get ahead of them.

This is because I view product and engineering to be a lot more related to group dynamics than anything else. An effective product and engineering organization isn't in the form of numbers, it's in the form of group dynamics. I've seen engineering teams with 50 people out-deliver engineering teams with 300 people and the reason that happens isn't because all those 50 people are the best of the best. It's because of the group dynamics. It is because of how they work together as an organization; it's because of how they deal with all the politics. It just naturally occurs whenever you have multiple people working together as well. Some of the best products and technical teams are good because they have good leaders and managers, not because they're incredibly technical. And a great leader is great at hiring A players, great at managing A players, and great at interpreting customer needs into solutions that are very aligned and thoughtful.

Just know that in evaluating the technical team, you will probably not have a lot of metrics and KPIs and the best way to evaluate the technical team is by understanding the CTO and the group dynamics.

8

How to Use the VCIF

By having a framework like the VCIF, you can take the many, many different data points you'll gather as you learn about startup opportunities and at least be able to place them into one of the six buckets to start. But the VCIF is just that—a starting point. For a lot of reasons, it will never be completely filled in. You're not going to get the chance to answer every single question you might have because you only have so much time and information. You may have answers to these six questions but there are multiple sub-questions and nuances around those that just require learning by doing.

In fact, the biggest constraint when it comes to evaluating an opportunity well is time—VCs never have all the time they need; instead, they want to figure out every factor within reason. With that time constraint, the reality is that, for almost every factor, you are required to lean on your experience. Some people call it "gut instinct," and others call it intuition. Every investment just requires it. There are some ways to be more efficient, for example, like talking to the founders' backchannel references but unfortunately, you still have to prioritize between the six questions and you have to prioritize how deep you go into each question of the VCIF.

But you should have an opinion about all six questions. For instance, for every investment, you should have an idea of the size of the market. The startup is not going to tell you the size of the market. They can give you their opinion but you'll have to make up your own mind. The team can tell you, "We're the best team in the world!" but you have to make up your own mind. Is it the best team in the world? And so everyone will (and should) apply the framework differently. Within every VC partnership there will be disagreements, disagreements in priority, disagreements on the grading, disagreements on timing, and so on.

You can think of the VCIF a little bit like a cheat sheet. It doesn't give you the answers and you still have to apply your thinking to it. But for an unstructured and growing industry like VC, it is so helpful to have a framework to help guide your conversations with startups or help you evaluate how good a company is because you at least know what the buckets are. The best way to demonstrate how to use the framework is by comparing two companies—one that we invested in and the other, one of the thousands of companies that we didn't invest in.

THE VCIF IN ACTION: AN INVESTMENT WE MADE

When we invested in this company it had already reached about $2 million in revenue and had about a dozen employees. We invested in the series B round, which is still an early-stage company, but they are further along than a pure startup. They have revenue, they have customers, they have a product, and what we're betting on when we invest in a series B is, "Hey, you have some initial momentum that you've already made, can you continue this momentum? Can this company one day become a very large business?"

Who

In using the VCIF framework, I'll just go through each question and discuss how it applies. So, for *Who*, the company hired a great team that was extremely skilled and was able to stay on with the business for five years as the company grew. And the importance of that is that the company didn't need to be up-leveled—they didn't need to spend time and money recruiting and interviewing candidates. Now, the CEO was a first-time CEO but they had the skills and experience to be a great CEO. The CMO was deeply skilled as a CMO and they scaled brilliantly. And the head of sales had never been head of sales before, but they also had all the skills. They were fundamentally good. They were thoughtful, they were skilled, and they were consistent.

What

The next bucket, *What*, addresses the problem this company was solving and the big problem at that time was that businesses had too much information. Businesses were just overloaded with information because, with our obsession with data and analytics, a lot of companies started providing reams of data to customers. Unfortunately, some of that data was very difficult to decipher and some of the customers didn't have the tools nor the resources to analyze it all and they ended up with false positives and other problems. What this startup focused on was reinventing that way of thinking about data and said, "Hey, what if we only gave you as little data as possible? But every time we gave you something, it was the highest, most valuable, most important data that was very actionable instead?" What this company did was enable a new technique, along with a new approach, to a big problem. The problem was there and it impacted businesses of every size in every industry.

When

The big data problem was a conversation that we talked about in the industry frequently in terms of *When*, in terms of timing. And timing was one of the key factors to focus on because the technique that the company developed was actually not brand new. The way they made the technology scale was new. The technique had been tried before but never took off in the past. It was mostly experimental and startups were created based on this technique but they didn't get very far. So timing was definitely a consideration and our concern was, "Hey, what's different now versus before that will make timing more interesting?" Timing is something that defines the nature of early-stage investing because you can't predict timing. You have to guess. You have to dig pretty deep to understand if the timing is right.

If we were to grade the first three factors, *Who*, *What*, and *When*, I'd say that I could conclude with certainty that team/who and problem/what would be graded at A or B, but timing/when, I couldn't tell you if it was an A, B, or something lower. That's just the uncertainty that you need to accept as an early-stage investor. Sometimes you think timing is as low as a C but it ends up being an A because things evolve; things change beyond our vision.

Where

Size of the market, or *Where*, was really interesting and like timing, this is also one of the factors that is difficult to determine in an early-stage company. If, for instance, this solution was a better, faster, cheaper iteration or improvement of something that already existed, then you know exactly how big that market is. For example, if someone wanted to create another social media company, you know exactly how big that market is, or if you wanted to create another

CRM software like Salesforce, you know exactly how big that market is. People have tried to solve the "too much data" problem before and the market wasn't very large for this startup's solution. If we invested in this company, we were making the bet that the market was going to become large. Unfortunately, making that kind of bet is just the nature of early-stage startups and sometimes you just don't know how big a market will become until you invest in it, until it starts to grow. This factor, like timing, is difficult to rate—is it a B because it could become a large market? Or maybe it's a C because it's been done before and wasn't that large in the past. Nearly any grade you give to this company for *Where* is pretty much a guess.

Why

The *Why*, or solution is one where we rated the company as a very clear, very easy A, but for two different dimensions. One dimension that is really important to consider is the competition: How does a company fare versus their competitors? Our technology evaluation led us to have a lot of confidence in this company because they had the best solution compared to their competitors, but they also had a phenomenal engineering team that would be able to continue to lead the category. The other dimension to consider is, how well does this solution fit the problem? Here our evaluation wasn't as clear because the category the company was in was one of many different solutions to the problem of too much data, false positives, and just overwhelming amounts of data.

For example, one way to solve the problem of false positives is that you try to analyze it and delete all the data you don't need. And you try different techniques like data science and machine learning and AI instead of rules-based analysis and statistical analysis. This company's solution was novel because they flipped the whole problem on its head and started looking for high fidelity, important data versus quantity of data. At that point in time, though, customers were still very comfortable with having too much data and they weren't looking for high-fidelity data versus low-fidelity data. They were looking for better ways to process large amounts of data. So this company had to develop its solution and go from a C-level solution to fit the problem so that it was a B-level solution, and then develop it even further to an A-level solution so they could have an IPO or be acquired.

How

And then, finally, when we think about *How*, we're asking how this company would be able to execute and scale. The *How* we rated an A because we knew the team was a great team with a long runway before running out of talent. In addition, though, the company was able to scale up both the sales and marketing team and the results that they were delivering when they were only a $2 million revenue company continued as they scaled up. The engineering team was an asset in scaling, too, and they were based in India with a phenomenal leader based there. That engineering team could scale from a small team to an incredibly large team very quickly, so the technical talent needs for the company were solved. The same was true for the sales and marketing side of the company because they were able to hire students out of college and train and develop them and then ramp them to become marketing experts and execute the marketing programs. On the sales side, the sales leader had been a salesperson before and they were great at hiring and managing salespeople. And so the company had all the skills there and the ability to scale quickly.

One of the reasons this company was successful is that they were able to both bring customers to embrace their solution, and they were also able to migrate their company to a new emerging category. During their scale-up, the company became one of seven competitors doing the same thing, all trying to solve the overloaded-with-data problem. Ultimately, they became the number one company in the category but, at the time, it still wasn't an A graded category. Our thinking was, it's a good category, it's a good solution, but it's not a perfect fit to the problem. The company was forced to make one more pivot to create a new category that was a better fit, where they took the solution that they had and scaled it to a new problem. The solution fit to the new problem was even better—they had achieved product-market fit—and that was one of the main reasons they got acquired by a public company.

AN INVESTMENT WE DIDN'T MAKE

Who

The VC industry defines a series B company as one that has at least $1 million of revenue and it has a team, a product, and a vision of what the company can become. A series B company has already achieved a level of success and the company is looking for additional funding to keep it going. On the *Who* front, if you have an A graded team, you're always going to get funding and if you're a B-level or even a C-level team, you can still get funded because people grow, improve their skills, and become better at managing their business.

If you're a series B company, it's still very realistic to get funding, but it just might take a little bit more fundraising work. It is very rare for a series B company to be funded if investors passed on them because of the team. Of course, you want an A-level team when you're investing, no matter what, but in terms of the importance of the *Who* factor, it's a little bit lower.

What

The second factor though, the *What*, is really important because the VC is thinking, "Hey, this company already achieved a certain level of success, but can they keep it going? Can they reach exponential growth?" This is where the "problem" is critically important because it has to be a problem that everyone has. At the series B level, the investor can form their own opinion on whether the *What* is a problem or not, and here is where the specialist investor, the person who knows an industry really well, can shine. As a specialist in an industry, you'll know if the problem is real, if it is important, if it's a problem that will be around for a long time. If you allow someone else to define the problem for you and allow someone else to convince you that this problem is important, you're taking a bit of a risk. I have a lot of respect for the entrepreneurs who have gotten to series B because they have generated a high level of success, which is amazing, phenomenal, and great, but I commonly will pass on a company if I don't agree with them that this is a really important problem.

When

And that's what leads to the very next factor, *When*, which is the timing. The importance of timing changes, based on the stage of investments. At later-stage investments, the impact of timing becomes a little bit less of a factor. If a company is already at $20 million revenue—beyond a series B company—you already know the market is there, the category is there. The main question to ask is, how big can the category get? But for a series B company, a company with less than $5 million in revenues, they haven't yet proved that the category should exist, will continue to exist, and will become a big market. And so timing is an important factor in the series B company.

What

Earlier I discussed the successful company that we did invest in, and in that example there were multiple other companies who tried to solve the data overload problem. They weren't very successful and many of them got to the series B level, they got to $5 million in revenues. And they got stuck because they couldn't make that next inflection point in terms of the growth of both their own organization as well as the growth of the category. And that's a problem in timing but similar to understanding the *What*, or the problem, VCs understand and evaluate timing based on their own experience. The big difference between a very early-stage company and a series B company is that the series B will have data they can share with the VC from customers, for example.

One of the important things to be evaluating when you look at reference customer data at the microscopic level is whether or not that data helps you understand the problem, but if you look at that customer data collectively, it can help give you a feel for the importance of timing. Timing is also a potential reason why we pass on a space, because it's very hard to predict timing. At a series B level, you basically have a developing company in a developing category and there are so many unknowns. If you don't have a strong opinion on the space and the company, then investing is a big risk. And this is one area where if you're wrong, you just cut your losses, move on, and think, "Maybe I'll invest in this company's series C instead, because I called it wrong on timing."

Where

Where, or size of the market, is one factor that is very important. It ties into the previous factors, like, is this an important problem? Is this the right time? But one other dynamic when you think about TAM is knowing what kind of investor you are. What exits are you seeking? If you're the kind of investor that says, "Hey, every single exit has to be an IPO, or it doesn't matter. It doesn't impact me, it doesn't drive my fund," then TAM is incredibly important. Obviously, *Where* is very important to the billion dollar fund because those VCs have to chase IPOs that will have incredibly large exits so that they can return the fund and generate the returns they need. If you are an investor that can only go after very, very large TAMS, then even if you find a really interesting opportunity, you will not invest in any company in the category. So one reason VCs pass on a company at the series B level is because they don't believe the TAM exists to generate the returns they need.

Why

Why, or the solution to the problem, is one factor where you can go really deep and, in fact, I think it's worth going deep. Understanding the solution is an area where you don't rely only on the company to tell you the answer, but you cast a wide net and talk with reference customers as well as backchannel references to customers to help form your own opinion. For example, let's say you believe in the problem, you believe in the timing, you believe in the market size, the next thing you need to believe in is that the solution is a good fit to the problem. Is there strong product-market fit? It's super-helpful to have your own opinion so you have a baseline hypothesis to work with, but it's also really important that you talk to customers and to everyone and anyone in the ecosystem. Your aim is to try to get a sense of how delighted they are, how satisfied they are by the solution, and how important it is for them as well.

Understanding the solution, for a series B company, is a place where diligence is really helpful and can either make or break your investment. We have passed on companies because where there was a real problem, the timing was right, and there was a really large TAM, but the solution wasn't the best fit for what was there.

How

The last factor, *How*, or scale asks how a company will continue building and growing this business. Of course, this is an important question to answer but your answer depends on what kind of investor you are. Are you the investor that enjoys jumping in and helping people hire and grow and scale, or are you the investor who says, "Hey, I invest in a lot of great markets and great teams and I allow them to execute and scale on their own?" There are two ways of thinking about coaching or managing, and every team is a little bit different and that's a dynamic that needs to be factored in. If you feel that a company needs help to scale but they don't want the help, or you don't see the ingredients already present within the company, that could impact you. It might not be enough of a reason to pass on the company, but it could be a reason to be less excited about that investment than other investments.

You do have to think about the fit of the investment with your style because it does calibrate the amount of excitement, and that's important in venture. If you find a team where you think, "Wow, they've already made a lot of progress. They're super-hungry, they're really easy to work with, they want the help and I can see exactly how I can help them," then you can feel much better about an investment. Your level of excitement, when it's all done, is important, and how excited are you about this opportunity? How optimistic are you about this company's success? That excitement and optimism factor into a whole new ballgame in venture which is valuing companies, deciding what are the terms you'd like to offer. That's a topic for another book, but ultimately your level of optimism about a company being successful, your excitement level about investing, are a dynamic to consider. So, it's not just the cut-and-dried answers you get doing your due diligence, there is also an emotional context as well.

STAGES

The examples I provided to illustrate the VCIF in action were both series B companies and one common theme running through both scenarios is that the framework is not completely filled in because of the stage of the company. There are some things you just cannot figure out with a series B or earlier-stage company. That's what makes venture risky and exciting. For example, there are scenarios where a founder comes to you and they have an idea that you believe is terrible. It's just a horrible idea that you don't think will be successful, but you respect the founder. You decide to suspend your disagreement and instead think, "Well, the founder knows more about this than me and even though I think it's a terrible idea, I'll still invest anyway." That could turn out to be a phenomenally good decision but what drives that decision? It's your belief in the founder, in the founding team.

In a startup, the team may have to change course completely and while people are important in every business, every group-based activity, in venture, the criteria will look a little bit different. Because when you're an early-stage company, you are not Goliath, you are David and no one knows you. The venture capitalist needs different skills, different mindsets, to be able to evaluate that. When it comes to startups and venture, you start having to think about the world a little bit differently, you think about the world from, "Hey, I want to be disruptive, I want to create something that hasn't been created before and I need to make the most of the little bit of funding that I do have." That mental mindset of a startup requires good people who then need to hire and identify great people. I feel very confident that the number one reason our early-stage companies grow to become later-stage successes is because of the team.

In the earlier stages there are some things in the framework that frankly aren't important—they can be at a lower priority. One of those is *How*, because it covers things like go-to market execution and in the early stages, there is no go-to market because there is no marketing team; there is no sales team. A lot of times, the founder is the salesperson and the first ten employees are engineers because you need to build something to sell something. You need to have a product that people can buy and put their hands on. The *How* comes into play when you hire a head of marketing, when you have between 20 and 30 employees, and you need to focus on breaking through the noise in the market.

Product is an example of something that's more important mid-stage to late stage rather than early stage when you have three people. Do they really have a product? Probably not, so there's nothing to evaluate. But, what's important at this early stage is whether or not there is a path to the product. How are they going to get to product-market fit, and can this team do it? If you look at VCs who invest in late-stage companies, you'll see that they apply the framework differently because they will have more data on each of the six questions.

In using the VCIF, there is nuance involved because you can get lots of data, but then you have to interpret the data. And that's where the nuance comes in. But the data is accessible, especially with late-stage companies that have customers, partners, vendors, and a track record. Using the framework can't be strict because you have to apply it differently based on the stage of the company. There is no way you will find a company that is A grade on everything. So you have to develop hypotheses, test them, and come to your own conclusions.

Part III

Notes
to Stakeholders

9

The Venture Capital Role

This Part is not meant to be a comprehensive summary of how venture capital works. That would deserve another book. If you have additional questions after these chapters, the best place to ask me is via LinkedIn. https://www.linkedin.com/in/linwilliam/.

After this book is published, I will continue to answer questions about VC and investing there.

The world of venture capital is often depicted in the news and social media as having millions and billions of dollars: multiple financing rounds (Series Seed, A, B, C, D, E, F, etc.), Initial Public Offerings (IPOs), and Merger and Acquisitions (M&A), or as unicorns—billion-dollar valuations of the latest high-flying startup destined to be the next Apple, Amazon, Google, Microsoft, or Netflix. And while a unicorn valuation is a relatively rare event, with the news constantly focused on them, it's easy to start viewing venture capital as unicorn spotters: finding the next important company that will change the world. One outcome that stems from venture capital's popularity in the media is that a lot of people are choosing not to work in traditional roles but aiming for venture capital instead. I made that choice myself over ten years ago—going from a traditional post-undergraduate investment banking role to venture capital—back when we needed to take a pay cut to do that. But I have no regrets about that career change because venture capital is a lot more than finding companies, investing in them, and watching them grow.

Venture capital is an important component in an ecosystem built around entrepreneurship, and impacts the lives of many people. It impacts the lives of the investors who are investing money and, more importantly, their futures in risky companies. It impacts everyone in the startup, from the founder down to the most junior person in the organization. It impacts customers, who now have access to a never-before-seen product or technology, or get a faster or cheaper solution for something that's important to them. It impacts suppliers and vendors, it impacts communities, and it impacts the economy.

Venture capital is a worthwhile pursuit, but it's not easy to understand—there's a lot of complexity, a lot of nuances in how investment decisions are made and why decisions are made, and there are a lot of factors, including some luck that could impact whether you will be a wildly successful VC or not.

THE BASICS OF A VENTURE CAPITAL FIRM

One of the easiest ways to think about venture capital is to compare it to other industries that deal with finance, investments, and returns. My background prior to venture was in investment banking so I'll use that as one way to think about venture, but the same comparisons could be made to private equity, hedge funds, or any other high finance industry.

Relatively speaking, venture capital is a young industry—about 50 years old, while banking has been around since at least 6000 BCE and investment banking came about during the Civil War, in the 1860s. One of the consequences of that is extreme volatility in venture capital compared to other finance sectors—there are a lot more ups and downs and the swings are much higher and much lower than other industries. There are times when venture capital and entrepreneurship are the hottest things in the world and there are times when people would like to invest in things that are less risky or more predictable than venture capital. And that volatility impacts all aspects of the venture industry.

Another big difference between most hedge funds/private equity and venture is how quickly returns on investment get captured by the firm. In venture, the timeline to capture return in a "winner" investment is measured in 5–10 years. In venture, a fund is constructed with a targeted 10-year life-cycle and the initial five years is when you do the investing and the second five years is when you are harvesting—you're not investing in new companies during those second five years. While hedge funds and private equity firms frequently realize their "winners" in five years or less, and, as a result, have a shorter time to return capital to their funds and subsequently to their investors, called Limited Partners (LPs). Table 9.1 presents some definitions of key terms in venture capital.

The venture capital fund is typically a combination of investors from the venture firm because they have to put skin in the game themselves, called the general partner (GP) commitment, and then the firm will look for LPs to invest in the fund. The venture firm will be investing the fund, consisting of both their GP commitment as well as their LPs' capital. The firm's goal is to generate returns within each fund and in exchange for managing the funds, the firm

Table 9.1 **Definitions of key terms in venture capital**

Term	Definition
General Partner (GP)	An employee of the venture capital firm who invests capital in the funds that the firm manages. These are typically the most senior leaders of the firm, responsible for fundraising with outside LPs in addition to their investment and managerial responsibilities.
Limited Partner (LP)	An outside investor who invests in funds for the purposes of financial returns.
Firm	A holding company that employs every employee, including investors and operational roles.
Fund	A pool of capital raised by the firm for the purposes of investment by the firm. The capital is raised from general partners and limited partners. Venture capital firms will raise multiple funds over time, typically every 2–3 years so that the firm can continue to make investments.
GP commitment	Typically expressed as a percentage of the fund size; this is the amount of capital the GPs collectively commit to invest personally.

collects a fee ranging from 1–3% of the fund's capital every year for about 10 years. The industry standard fee varies and is typically undisclosed, but it's a good approximation of fund expenses. Expenses include operations, offices, salaries, bonus, travel, accountants, due diligence, lawyers, and anything else that comes up as a normal business expense. The vast majority of venture capital funds also have an equity structure which is valuable when (or if) the fund returns all of the capital invested and fees (this is called a "European waterfall"). This equity is called "carry" and the equity component is similar to a startup: typically, the investors who take more risk by joining an organization earlier and the more senior investors participate in the equity. It's because of these dynamics and many others that venture is not a "get-rich-quick" industry. In fact, this helps to explain why it is so common for successful, wealthy CEOs to transition to VC in their later careers. They have sufficient net worth where their GP commitment can be significant.

People don't just give VCs money—it's never the case that somebody just walks up to a VC firm and wants to invest in one of their funds. In a process that feels eerily similar to founders raising capital from VCs, VCs also have to work to raise capital from LPs. Fortunately, there is a large ecosystem that limited partners are involved in. There are multiple conferences that are just for limited partners and one of the biggest life lessons I learned while spending time with LPs, who were managing and deploying hundreds of millions to billions per year, was that it made me realize that there is a lot of wealth that people throughout the world have generated and they're trying to figure out how to invest it. There's a phrase I heard at one of these limited partners conferences that really stuck with me and that is that there are people who are trying to get rich and then there are people who are trying to stay rich. Limited partners are trying to figure out, "Hey, how do I generate more value from this capital so I can continue to make good use of this capital? Because if I just let it sit around, it's going to get gradually eaten away by inflation." Many limited partners have amazing causes, right? Like they are not just trying to make money to buy more yachts or vacation homes, they also have the intent to make the world a better place with their capital through philanthropy and other commitments to society. I personally like limited partners who come from universities, for example, because some of the earnings they get from investing are going to be put toward scholarships and students, and professors' salaries, and research. There are a lot of good reasons to be a limited partner in a fund but you really can't be a limited partner unless you already have the wealth to invest. LPs are managing lots of pools of capital and they're responsible for figuring out how to invest capital in a way that works best for them in a mixture of funds (debt, real estate, private equity, hedge funds, venture capital, etc.) and also directly into various asset classes. This is diversification at the highest scale, measured in the hundreds of billions with the largest LPs. And the criteria LPs use to evaluate whether or not they're making the impact they want may range from performance to sectors they are interested in to alignment to their mission.

For example, LPs might be motivated by causes, like scholarships for underrepresented minorities, or they may have a thesis that is driving their investment decisions. Perhaps they're focused on breakthrough cancer research, or maybe they see food security as a global issue and want to use their funds to address that. It's also possible that an LP will have strong opinions on sectors or markets that they want to avoid, like the tobacco industry, for example. The point is, there is not a one-size-fits-all LP and they are as differentiated and nuanced as everything else in venture, and that's why you'll see many, many different funds and approaches and why, also, it's not as easy to find LPs for a fund as people assume. It's not a matter of just finding or knowing people with capital who want to deploy it. There are a lot of drivers that go into finding alignment between investors and funds and companies.

So one part of venture capital is creating and managing these funds, and the other part is investing, and both parts are impacted by the broader economy; both are cyclical. When markets are good, it is easier to raise money; if interest rates are low, it's easier to raise money; if people get a windfall, then it's easier to raise money. Starting in about 2016 or a year or two earlier, the economy has been good in terms of underlying conditions, but there are other factors besides the overall economy, like supply and demand, that also come into play and impact venture. Supply of funding opportunities is easier in a growing economy, but demand is also higher. I would say that of the two, fundraising or investing, generally, the more difficult task is investing itself, because there are far more people who have failed at investing than fundraising. The reality is, in venture, not that many people get the opportunity to even fundraise because many investors typically join a fund that has already raised capital.

WINNERS LOSE A LOT

The reality of venture capital is that winners lose a lot. In a fund, the greatest investments create all the returns but there are a lot of losers. In venture, we refer to that as the "power law." There are certain deals that make the fund super-successful and there are other deals that aren't that critical or impactful. The more risk-accepting VCs have to be comfortable with the high loss ratio that really defines the nature of venture capital. The loss ratio means that, out of all the money you've invested, how much of it goes to zero? How much of it do you just lose completely? A loss ratio that's common in venture capital is about 50% (even some really great funds have loss ratios between 35% and 70%) and that's accepted by people in the industry.

That's why the winning investments are so important because the winners make up for everything else. And both the winners and losers are in the same fund because a fund can have 20 companies, for instance, and not all of those 20 companies will be winners. One common method and metric of thinking about winners and investing in companies is thinking about VC funds that are capable of "returning the fund." And what I mean by "returning the fund" is that if one or several companies in a fund have enough success to cover the losses of all the other investments, then we say the fund is returned. That means that all of the capital invested is made up and LPs are made whole. After that, every investment feels like "house money" and you are also "in carry" and beginning to keep 20% of the profits (assuming the fund has 20% carry). And the most common way to measure a potential fund returner is called a "unicorn," a company valued at a billion dollars or above.

So, the unicorns get all the media attention, but there are venture capitalists who are consistently hitting numbers well below that billion dollar valuation and providing incredible returns to their investors. At the end of the day, if a fund is returning three to five times the return to their investors, they are amazing. But not all investors invest in a company in the earliest stages, so your returns also depend on what the valuation is when you jump in. That part is just math. Earlier-stage investors typically invest in startups when they are riskier at lower valuation and thus enjoy a greater ROI when a portfolio company exits, compared to the later-stage investor who invested at a higher value.

One term used in venture is "vintages," which refers to time periods during which a 10-year fund starts to invest capital. The reason why this exists is because markets go through ups and downs, and it is sometimes difficult to compare investments that you've made in, let's say, 2010, versus investments that you made in 2020. Those are two completely different markets—different macroeconomic environments, different companies, different technologies, different issues—they are completely different. There are some markets where everything is so depressed but you ride it out and then it goes straight into a bull market where it's very hard not to make money. You can have a situation where you invested at a valuation based on 3x revenue ("revenue multiple"), for example, and then get to sell the business for a 10x revenue multiple because the markets are better and the markets are higher; you've already made this fantastic return. Because of the different shifting market conditions, what LPs do is they benchmark companies by their vintage, so if one fund is started in 2012, an LP will compare returns to all other funds started in 2012. It is an apples-to-apples comparison. When you think about the history of all investing in all venture capital, private equity, hedge funds, and every investment vehicle, if you are consistently returning at least three times the capital, you are one of the best investors in the world.

Another key difference venture has with other financial roles is the involvement of the investors with the company (Table 9.2). In most of finance, the relationship is based on the numbers, not so much the product, team, or market. In venture, you can expect a lot of ups and downs and it requires the successful venture capitalist to have a lot of patience because things never happen as quickly as you want them to. On top of that, optimism comes into play, because if you let the downs really take you down, then you're going to struggle. We are influencers, at the end of the day, of the company. There are very few situations where a venture capitalist is the decision-maker—and that's a good thing, because if we were the key decision-maker on some crucial decisions, or we needed to be involved in everyday decisions, that would be a situation that just would take too much time and doesn't scale. Yes, we can be on a startup's board; yes, we can use our networks to provide introductions to people who can help them scale; yes, we can be a sounding board; and, yes, we can have extensive experience with a lot of the issues that a founding team

Table 9.2 **Comparison of investment styles**

Investment style	Private equity buyout	Venture capital	Hedge fund
Typical involvement	Highest	Medium	Lowest
Duration	< 5 years	Early stage: >5 years Late stage: <5 years	Depends on strategy

is going to face—but we're not the entrepreneurs. We're not the decision-makers, we're not the ones who have the vision. The role of the venture capitalist requires a lot of patience, it requires a lot of trust. And it requires a lot of optimism because, in some ways, you are the cheerleader for each company you invest in.

And that really is the key difference between venture and every other high finance industry: the venture capitalist needs to work with the entrepreneur and their fellow board members. VCs need to be vested in the team, product, and market. We are humans, too, and so are the founders, the board, and so are the CEOs of the companies and all the C-suite people. At the end of the day, we need to be able to work together as humans. So I do find myself thinking as a VC in this role, "How do I improve my communication skills? How do I communicate my thoughts here in a productive way? How do I make sure that I don't say things in an accusatory way where founders feel marginalized or become defensive?" Working with entrepreneurs, helping them bring their vision to the world, is the key differentiator between venture and all other high finance jobs. If you are thinking about venture as a career, then working with entrepreneurs should be the top criterion you use to determine if this is a career for you. Everyone has different ideas about what they like and what's important to them, but for me the idea of creating, being near creation, or helping with creation feels very empowering.

METRICS

One of the questions every venture capitalist faces is, what is a good company? What defines it? You might think that if a company is growing well, if employees are motivated and getting paid, and if they have paying, happy customers, it's a "good" company. And the reality is, that does sound like a good company! But from a VC's perspective, we do need a consistent metric to compare companies and to pattern match companies. One simple metric which has become the default, as companies are increasingly using a subscription-based model, is annual recurring revenue (ARR), which is a measure of recurring revenue growth. Three to five years ago, the industry used annual contract value (ACV) or total contract value (TCV) as the critical metric, and three to five years before, that it was GAAP (generally accepted accounting principles) revenue.

Today, in the 2020s, the metric is ARR. Using ARR as a metric has its pros and cons and it mostly applies to companies that have a specific business model—a subscription model or a usage model. There are many companies that use a subscription model—not just startups—and even Fortune 500 companies have tried to create subscription or usage models. For example, 20 years ago if you bought a Windows-based PC, it most likely came with the Windows operating system and you could use that computer indefinitely and the Microsoft products like Word, Excel, and PowerPoint were additional purchases but also lifetime licenses. Those days, GAAP revenue was the best metric to measure success, as once the software sale was made, revenue could be recognized soon after.

Today, that's not the case and if you want to have the suite of Microsoft products, it is much more common to pay a yearly subscription fee. We also saw iconic companies like Adobe transition their Photoshop software into a recurring subscription fee, complete with software, services, and storage. While public companies like Microsoft have managed to take a one-time purchase and turn it into an annual revenue stream, another model companies have used is a tiered system with "free" as one option for basic services and going up from that to monthly or annual pricing model.

MY FIRST TRIAL BY FIRE

The first company I ever looked at as a new investor in venture capital was a fascinating experience for me and I have come to learn that my experience is not all that unique. It actually is representative of what many VCs experience when they do due diligence on their first company as well. That first experience is also a lesson in how venture works, what you ought to expect if you join a VC firm, and how your work—even with the very first client—can be impactful. It also highlights the need for a framework, like the Venture Capital Investment Framework, so that an entry-level person can build the confidence that they are asking the right questions as they conduct their due diligence.

The first company I invested in and carried out due diligence for was a company called Fruition Partners, based in Chicago. They are a services company that helps customers deploy ServiceNow, which is an enterprise management system, and also a way for people to build applications on top of ServiceNow. Fruition Partners became one of the preferred partners for ServiceNow to deploy their software, and, as a result, Fruition Partners had an exponential growth rate of 500% over one year. The way that Fruition Partners works is that they train students right out of college on how to deploy ServiceNow and then send them into the field to deploy it on behalf of customers.

Where Fruition really shines is that they have two drivers of their business. On the sales side, being a preferred partner for ServiceNow means that they get a lot of business from ServiceNow, but also Fruition has their own reputation and direct sales. Fruition has the ability to go out externally and say, "Hey, I see that you're trying to deploy ServiceNow. You don't have the people yourself to install it. Let us do it for you." Fruition Partners has those two balancing functions, sales and delivery, and that's why they had phenomenal growth.

For me, I did not know any of this when I started with my due diligence of Fruition. I didn't know why they grew. I didn't know how they're delivering the value that they were delivering. And I didn't know the components that were necessary for high returns in a business like Fruition's. It was definitely a trial by fire learning experience for me, because the way it worked was that I was paired with an experienced partner who asked all the questions that he needed answered to make a decision that he felt comfortable with to invest in Fruition. He had so many questions that Fruition set up a data room, a place where the company provided the data that answered most of the questions the partner asked. The partner created the agenda of when we would go on site, who we should meet, who we should interview, how much time we want to spend with each person—all those meetings and research were decided by the partner, and I tagged along.

And the part where I could jump in and I could transfer my skills from investment banking straight into venture capital was in building a financial model for Fruition Partners. I was able to look at Fruition's historical financials and I was able to project what Fruition's future financials could look like. If we tweaked something, if we spent more money here or if we took some action, I was able to analyze the business in an operational way, but from a financial perspective. A lot of my experience, and what made venture so interesting, was seeing all this data, hearing all these questions and being totally clueless and having to figure out, what is going on? Why are these questions being asked? What does this data mean? Why did we ask this question during one of these interviews? What is a good answer? Is that a good answer? I don't know. I have no idea. It sounds like a good answer, but how can I tell?

My trial by fire required a lot of independent guessing and thinking and it required me to look at all the data, to look at all the questions that this partner asked and to think, okay, is this a good answer to the question that was asked, based on my experience of understanding businesses from the financial side? And those questions I had, I turned into questions that I could ask the partner, like, "Hey, partner, this looks good. Do you agree? Hey, partner, this looks bad. Do you agree?"

And asking these questions actually ended up being very net positive because I could look at all the data from a fresh perspective and ask questions that wouldn't normally be asked. And some of those questions ended up being dumb and I figured out on my own, okay, this was not a good question to ask. But some of those questions ended up being innovative and useful and helpful, and questions that people sometimes just don't ask because they already assume the answers. So in that way, it became really valuable.

Even though I felt like I knew a lot about finance, this is when I learned even more because the skills you bring from investment banking are very akin to skills that you might bring from a hedge fund, like modeling how the three financial statements work with each other. And if you spend more on sales and marketing, this is how much more revenue that you get, for example. But what I didn't have experience doing was something like revenue recognition, where you look at every single contract related to every single customer, and you figure out, if the customer committed to spending $5 million over five years, how does that

$5 million convert into a revenue gap in the financial statements? Questions like that actually required me to learn how to be an auditor, like an accountant. These were things that I sort of knew how to do, but I had never applied these skills in the real world to an actual company.

This gave me the opportunity to go through every single contract and then to build a model that said, okay, this is what the revenue will be in one month from now, based on these existing contracts that have already been booked. This is what the revenue will be one quarter from now or one year from now based on what's already been booked. And then it allowed me to build another model, which is, okay, this is the revenue that will be booked and this is how that new revenue is going to be recognized as well. And that allowed me to be able to predict what were all the different inputs that are required for this company to go, for instance, from $12 million to $40 million, and how much time it would take.

One other operational skill that I learned from doing this diligence was the management of people. For example, in most companies and organizations, we have the typical 40-hour work week, but people don't actually work for the full 40 hours. Yes, they're on the clock for 40 hours, but are they actually working all 40 hours? That's not sustainable. Because people have to take some breaks. And that's when I learned about this concept of utilization rates, which basically asks, out of all the time that a person is clocked in, how much of that time is being applied to customer-facing value? How much of that time is being applied to being on the bench while they're waiting for the next project? And how much of that time is being spent on vacations and holidays? How much of that time is being spent on training and learning? And what happens in terms of the utilization rate of course is that during the first couple of months when a new employee, fresh out of college, joins Fruition, their utilization rate was very low because they had to do a lot of training to prepare for the services they would be providing to customers.

After a certain amount of time, that's when they would become fully productive and then after more time and experience, that's when they got to start doing higher-level functions where we could charge more money per hour. But all of this information about utilization rates, for example, I learned on the fly. When we did our onsite and we were interviewing the head of Human Resources, I had zero experience with HR, so when my partner asked the question, "Hey, what is the biggest bottleneck in the company right now?," my response was, "Whoa, that's a great question!" The bottleneck right now is that they don't have the money, they don't have the resources, so if we give them the money, what bottlenecks can get unlocked, according to you, dear head of talent?

They would sometimes talk about talent needs, but sometimes they'd talk about things completely outside of their scope. They'd be like, "Oh, you know what? If we have more funding, we'll actually be able to do more marketing." And when you hear the finance person talking about marketing, the talent person talking about marketing, and the salesperson talking about marketing, you're like, okay, marketing is probably a real bottleneck in the company and a lot of people agree with that.

Beyond some of the details of how I applied my investment banking background to do diligence on Fruition Partners, this experience also gives a sense of why the venture industry is still very much a mentorship industry. And the reason why is that there are so many things you cannot learn until you're actually doing a transaction, until you're actually digging into a company, and until you're listening to an experienced partner unpack the data and ask the questions of others. And my perspective is that if you do 20 deals in one year, that is far more valuable than doing 20 deals over three years. Why? Because the most important thing, and this is my bias, is that the best learning comes from experience.

This is why I love venture capital. This is why I love entrepreneurship. Most people have to learn by doing because we don't have books available. We don't have many classes available to us. And there are just some nuances that you can only learn by seeing it first-hand. Venture is very much a drinking from the fire hose industry—there is a lot of information thrown at you and you're expected to deal with it and make a recommendation. As a result, the people who get that opportunity to drink from the fire hose, especially early VCs, often comment, "I can't believe they're letting me do this. I can't believe they're depending on me to do this work because I've never done this before and this is an important decision. I can't believe they're letting me do it."

One of the things that we have to recognize about the dynamics of venture is that it is a black box, and this industry does feel like drinking from a fire hose. The whole motivation for me to write this book and share the Venture Capital Investment Framework is to make the venture industry feel less like a fire hose in some ways. And I hope that with this book, that readers can position themselves to be in the right place at the right time, so that they can either become a successful entrepreneur or they can become a successful venture capitalist, or get the opportunity to join a venture capital firm.

The aim of this framework is to help people be prepared, to help people deal with imposter syndrome, and help people find a structure to investing in venture capital. And I hope that this is at least a field guide that can be used as a starting point. You can become an expert where this field guide is intuitive, where in fact you can produce your own field guide in your own style and your own way. But the aim of the field guide is to give someone a starting point that they can develop or refine it themselves.

10

Notes for Students

THREE ENTRY-LEVEL CAREER PATHS IN VENTURE

When most people start in venture capital, they are asked to primarily help with three buckets of responsibilities: financial due diligence, market due diligence, or they are asked to help in what is often called "sourcing" or "scouting," i.e., identifying companies and entrepreneurs to invest in, more of a sales or business development role. A useful way to think of these three pathways to venture capital is to look at the tools that we use: Excel, PowerPoint, and a customer relationship management (CRM) system like Salesforce. Over-generalizing, investment banking candidates' differentiated superpowers are in Excel, consulting candidates are able to make PowerPoint sing, and people with a sales background are masters at keeping the CRM machine dancing.

If you come from consulting, you'll be tasked with figuring out how big is this market and who else is in this market, and how are they competing with each other? What are the trends related to this market? Another is looking for people who can help with actually "sourcing" or finding companies to invest in and filling the investment firm's pipeline with opportunities to consider.

I had an economics background and came from investment banking, so, in my first days at the firm I was most often working in Excel and modeling scenarios. For example, I would analyze situations where, if the company sells for $200 million, how much does every equity holder make? And by doing all that math, eventually I was able to understand the motivations for all the different investors because, if we get philosophical and believe we are in a capitalist society, each person is aligned to optimize the amount of money that they'll make. As VCs, when we decide to make that next investment, one way we can decide the valuation of the company is by looking at the return the company will make and then we can say, "We think this company could sell between $400 and $600 million in the future." So, if we value the company at between $100 and $200 million, then we can see the ROI that we'll make on this investment. And when we model all of the different details, we eventually can conclude, "Okay, this is a high-risk investment so we need to make sure that we make more than 3x, we need to make sure we make 5x or maybe 10x if things go really, really well." The classic risk/reward balance.

By working in Excel and doing the modeling, I started to understand the motivations of VCs, especially on the monetary side. One of the first things was understanding things like return on invested capital (ROI) and internal rate of return (IRR), and seeing that the longer we're holding this company, the more we should be making. I started seeing preferences so that if we were an investor in a company for two years, we should make 2x, and if we hold the company for three years, we should make 3x, if we hold for four years we make 4x, and so on. I understood that there's a nice trend or alignment between both time/IRR and ROI.

But understanding the numbers on the investing side didn't help with one of my big struggles and that was, how is anybody trusting the VCs to be investing large sums of money in a high-risk situation? For example, let's say we're making a relatively small investment, a $10 million investment in a company. I myself have nowhere close to $10 million in my bank account, but why is anyone trusting me or our firm? And some people make $100 million investments, but how do people feel comfortable deploying these huge amounts of money in a risky startup? It took me some time to gain my own self-confidence to be able to work with such large sums of money, but it also took me some time to understand the privilege of being in venture capital, where we have the opportunity to be able to invest such large amounts of money. It made me think a lot about why this industry exists and how people feel so comfortable deploying these enormous sums of money. And then I wondered, is the venture capital industry actually a productive one? Are people actually creating value? Are the investors in venture capital firms actually generating returns for their investors and how much are they making? Is it worth it?

My initial role was very numbers-oriented; my superpower was numbers and dollars, but it helped me see the different alignment decision points and reasons for doing what we're doing, why we're making some investments and passing on others. For instance, one of the things you'll do if you're conducting financial due diligence is compare similar companies. For example, if Series A companies are usually valued between $10–25 million (in the 2010s) and the venture capital industry has data that justifies this range of Series A, your job in due diligence is to decide if that $10–25 million valuation should be applied to the company you are researching as well. Having access to those numbers, using them to create models and scenarios, really helped me understand this ecosystem in a very rational way. The issue is, these numbers are all private and even if you happen to be a wealthy individual investor, or an Angel investor going it alone, you cannot get the quantity of data that active VCs naturally get from evaluating multiple Series A deals, for example. You will always be at a disadvantage compared to a venture firm and that is one reason why wealthy people invest in VC funds, because of the asymmetry in information and data.

After working in the financial due diligence role, primarily working on the numbers with Excel, I then started doing more research and due diligence that would be shown via PowerPoint. And what I mean by that is, while developing the PowerPoint skills, you're starting to write down insights that you find while doing interviews with people, or after polling people in the ecosystem, and basically doing work that is more in line with a consulting background, rather than a finance background. PowerPoint is a good way to move outside the numbers and move a little bit more into the qualitative aspects of venture capital. It's not fully qualitative, but a little more qualitative. PowerPoint tells a story and answers questions that people in VC are going to ask. So if you say to the senior partners, "Here is a CEO and I like their background," they might respond, "OK. So this person worked at Amazon for 20 years, and now they're starting a company. What did they do at Amazon? Do they actually have an entrepreneurial mindset or are they a big company person?" That's a good question and you'd better have an equally good answer to that. PowerPoint is a good opportunity for a junior person to start understanding the questions that VCs ask when they do their own due diligence about a company, a team, a product, or a space. And the reason why it's so helpful is that you use the slides as a way to guide the conversation beyond the numbers, beyond ROI. It's a different way of thinking about, and expressing, an opportunity but it is absolutely necessary in venture capital to have both the hard numbers and a logical explanation to go along with those numbers.

The third entry path to venture capital is the sourcing path, and for these folks their tool of choice is a CRM platform like Salesforce, Affinity, Hubspot, or any number of other platforms. This third path is all focused on identifying companies that you want to talk to. Finding ways to get in touch with them, finding ways to learn more about them, or finding the ones that you want to bring up to your team. You want to be able to say to your senior team, "Hey, here are some interesting opportunities and we should consider doing more diligence and potentially investing in this company." Officially the role looks a lot like the Business Development Rep (BDR) or the Sales Development Rep (SDR) role. The cynical way of phrasing the BDR role is to say that it's smiling and dialing because you are always on the phone, always emailing entrepreneurs to talk about their business, while the SDR role is primarily focused on helping to manage the inbound opportunities that come into a firm. The way that you represent all of this work in this third path is in the CRM.

Each venture capital firm is a little bit different in what type of initial starting point, in what kind of background they want from their entry-level VCs. And usually the venture capital companies that are in the earlier stage are looking for someone to help answer the questions, they are looking for people who are really skilled in PowerPoint. As a venture capital firm grows and moves to a later stage where they have more revenue and more data, they often have way more financials to crunch and that's when they usually look for entry-level VCs with an investment banking background and excellent Excel skills. Large venture capital firms with armies of associates might have all three backgrounds but are also commonly building their competitive advantage by having a large bench of sales skills. What I've seen happen with large, mature venture capital firms is that they tend to bifurcate into two main activities: sourcing and financial due diligence, and they look for people with either of those skills.

In my journey moving from Associate to Senior Associate, to VP, Principal, Partner, and then eventually to Managing Director, I had to build my skills in all three of these roles. I tried my hand at Excel, at PowerPoint, and CRM and I had to become proficient in all three to progress in my career as a venture capitalist. But they weren't all easy for me, especially the CRM role. I had a really tough time doing the sales part of the role, because you call an entrepreneur and let's say that they decide to talk to you. What I really want to learn is how well the company is doing and if I don't know the industry, the best way to measure how well a company is doing is to look at their revenue. And if I ask an entrepreneur, "What was your revenue last year?," many times they will not feel comfortable telling you that. So then the next question is, "Oh, what's your head count?" because you can use head count as a way to estimate their expenses. Then based on how profitable the company likely is, you can use algebra to approximate how much revenue they have. But nearly every entrepreneur knows that you're fishing for something and they don't know you and they're likely to not tell you anything. So what do you do? What am I selling? What am I telling them beyond just saying, "Hey, I'm with a venture capital firm and I have $700 million. Do you want to work with me?" There's no differentiation in that and so the sourcing part of venture capital was very difficult for me in the earliest days.

11

Notes for Current VCs

VC CAREER PATHS

What helped me the most in all three aspects—the numbers, the questions that we answer in the PowerPoint, and in the sales part—was building a perspective or expertise in a space. My one piece of advice for anyone going into venture capital is, the sooner you find a specialization that you want to spend time in, the more expert you become in a space, the more successful you will be. With deep knowledge of an area, it will be easier to create a great career path in a venture capital firm. By focusing and specializing in a space, two things happen: first, you become skilled at understanding and asking the right questions of the entrepreneurs that you meet; and, second, you are able to demonstrate to the entrepreneurs, "Hey, you don't have to teach me your space. I already understand your space and talking with me isn't going to be a waste of your time, but a great brainstorming opportunity. Let's build a relationship." And if you can build that relationship with entrepreneurs, then you can convince your firm to invest in a company and it becomes much more of a two-way street.

Without that specialization, you're stuck making phone calls or emailing everyone under the sun. I've always struggled with emails. Is it all about the email? Do I just email everyone or do I customize an email? What do I write in the email? Do I write about all the successful previous investments that we've done? Do I talk about how much money our fund is investing? Do I email the person that I know, "Hey, you are in the DC area and I happen to be in DC and would you want to meet because I happen to be there?" I started thinking through all the different sales tactics that people use, because I essentially became a salesperson and I was looking at conversion rates. If I email this to a bunch of companies, I might get a 50% response rate. But the issue with sales is that you can be busy forever and you can generate some leads but eventually, if you keep playing the different tricks, the games, and the tactics, you start getting some traction as well. But for sales, it doesn't matter what you do, or how much effort you put in, because it doesn't matter until the deal is closed. That's all that really matters.

If you have terrible metrics but you still win deals and you win more deals than people who have better numbers, that's all that matters. I was playing the numbers game but I just didn't know how to keep getting the numbers better and better and better. And I started thinking about other VCs who seemed to be getting deals done, and I just naturally assumed that was because they were more charismatic than I was, or because they were smarter than me. And I was wrong about that: I realized that it wasn't about selling or cold-calling, or the title that I used in my emails, or the number of deals we had done. It was about connecting with entrepreneurs in a way where we could have an authentic conversation, where we wanted to develop a long-term win-win relationship.

I distinctly remember the key inflection in my ability to build relationships. I was helping to start a cybersecurity-focused venture capital firm and a mentor suggested I take a class on cybersecurity to learn the fundamentals. And when

I started learning those fundamentals, that's when I started understanding the language that entrepreneurs in cybersecurity speak. And that's when I started realizing, "Oh, my gosh, I can actually have real conversations with these entrepreneurs now, I actually have a perspective and can provide it to them. I can have a discussion with them where the real thoughtful content doesn't run out 5 minutes or 10 minutes, which is basically bullet points or thoughts that I took from previous conversations; I can have a full one-hour conversation that is deep, thoughtful, and clearly demonstrates that if we work together, it could be an experience where we can learn something from each other. With expertise in an area I know what matters and I can actually contribute to their company and help them be successful." So one thing that really did jumpstart my career or catalyzed the next stage of my career was forming a perspective on an industry and on the problems facing that industry. This is the most frequent mentorship advice I share with up-and-coming VCs.

There are other ways to develop your career, too. The nice thing about sales, for example, is that you can look at it in terms of numbers—you can look at it in terms of results. What many junior investors tend to start with is the numbers, the financials, and they get comfortable with the numbers first. And then after getting really good with numbers, the journey starts to diversify. Some Next-Gen VCs will get really deep on thesis building, which is thinking about the market size, for example; other VCs will get really deep in networking with entrepreneurs, which is spending time and focusing on the team. And some up-and-coming VCs will continue down this path around sales where they will build a scalable sales machine for them to start bringing the numbers to the firm. All three of these paths work really well for a person's journey in venture because, essentially, all three roles are really focused on sourcing, or finding the companies to invest in. For the Next-Gen VC, it's a question of, are you proactively sourcing based on a thesis? Are you proactively sourcing based on the team? Or are you proactively sourcing based on numbers, where you are trying to talk to as many people as possible? For many Next-Gen VCs, you'll find that there are some elements of a role that are easy and other roles that are more challenging, like CRM and sales (for me). When I was on the Excel side, I was naturally good at financial analysis because of my investment banking experience. There was a learning curve coming from investment banking and going to venture capital, but I could look at examples of prior analyses for other companies, and I could understand why we had done a particular analysis and I could apply the same thinking to a company or problem that I was answering. Excel and PowerPoint were relatively easy because as investment bankers, we do spend a lot of time in PowerPoint. We are consolidating a lot of data, doing analytics to generate answers, and putting it all together to create a story.

The biggest challenge for me, starting out in venture, was that I knew what a good end state looked like, I just didn't know which questions needed to be answered to get to that good outcome. And so that part I learned by doing; I learned by listening to my firm and the questions the senior partners asked, I listened to the questions my mentors asked, and then I tried to understand why those questions were being asked. What were these senior people, mentors, and experienced VCs really trying to understand? If I heard a question get asked six times, I would conclude that this is probably an important question. Or, if I heard an answer 20 different times, I would conclude that this is probably what a truthful answer looks like. It didn't feel very efficient to me because I didn't know what "good" or "bad" looked like, and when I was sourcing deals and bringing companies into the firm, I had a hard time deciding which ones to bring up. Which ones really matter? Because as a Next-Gen VC, I'm not going to be the one joining the board and investing the time in making the startup successful. My job was to find the companies, help with diligence—financial and qualitative—on the good ones and then bring them to senior leadership.

So if I say to the partners, "Hey, I talked to 50 companies last week and here are the two that I think are worthy of conversation," that's going to set a lot of things in motion and shift the firm's resources to the opportunities I suggested. Early in my VC career, I wasn't very good at that and I made a ton of mistakes because I didn't know the difference between a good company and a bad company. It sounds obvious, it sounds like you should know what is good and what is bad, but I struggled with that. I would look at a company and think, "This company has so much revenue, it must be a good company." But it could be low-quality revenue. Maybe the company went from 5 to 100 employees, which looks great but it could be temporary and just as easy to lose. Early on I was just bringing up deals left and right and I would tell the partners, "I really liked this meeting," or this entrepreneur, or this is a company that's really exciting and interesting, and then people would do the diligence and come back to me and say, "It's actually not that great for this reason and that reason." It wasn't until I got lots and lots and lots of data that I could start finally being able to understand why those questions even mattered.

Winning deals in venture capital means there's a transfer of money in the opposite direction: we are giving startups money.

The one area where I struggled the most by far was in sourcing, with getting the deals. Venture capital, like other service industries—accounting, consulting, investment banking, or law—is driven by people who can get deals done. If you want to become the top producer in any of those industries, you have to be winning deals. You have to be finding and winning deals and, for many people, that's a very hard transition from providing a service to one day having to find customers and win their business. Venture capital is exactly the same as any of these other industries. In the initial days, you are providing leverage to the senior people. The senior people don't have the time or the interest to be crunching the numbers or to be doing the PowerPoint slides; they don't have time to write memos or have initial conversations with entrepreneurs. They hire people to provide leverage, to do those things, to crystalize the goodness and then give that to the more senior people to work with. And at the end of the day, for all of us, our time is our biggest constraint. It's nearly impossible for one person to call 200 companies, but it's very easy or realistic for 50 people to call 200 companies. If you hire more people, you can get more scale, more coverage and provide leverage to that venture capital firm. As a junior VC, you are providing leverage to the senior VCs, but to progress, you need to be winning deals and winning deals in venture capital is so different from winning deals in investment banking or consulting or accounting, or in law.

Winning deals in venture capital means there's a transfer of money in the opposite direction, where we are giving them money. And the nature of that deal also looks a lot like a marriage: We're on their board for the long term and for entrepreneurs, it's a lot like a shotgun wedding. They want to make sure they hire the right person to join their board. They want someone with the right culture, with the right working style, with the right skills that complement what the board needs. So, in many ways, the founders are hiring their board members and it is a big step, a big leap into the unknown. That's one of the things that makes venture capital so inspiring: we are investing in and working closely with some of the most talented entrepreneurs in the world, on what can be an unpredictable journey. It is extremely difficult to win a deal with an entrepreneur, and gratifying when you do win the trust of founders.

VC CAREER MYTHS

Although I have outlined the three pathways to venture capital, I get asked by people who are not in the industry what skills they should have or what background they need to get into venture. There's a myth that you have to be steeped in venture capital skills to get a job in venture capital, or that you have to be highly technical to get into the industry. Neither of those are true. For example, I studied computer science in college and majored in economics, which are helpful disciplines because of the analytical and critical thinking required, but I never took a course on venture capital and I don't believe that a venture capital course is a requirement for success in the industry. I have friends who took a course on venture capital, including my life-partner, so I have a sense of what that class entails and which textbooks are used. I have found that a lot of VC textbooks are focused on the tactical elements of venture capital. Most of the textbooks cover topics like how you fundraise, or how a firm is structured, or how to calculate a liquidation waterfall. These are all interesting tidbits to know or skills to have and if I were to hire an associate to join our firm, I would love it if they knew how to calculate a liquidation waterfall chart. That's amazing—that's a great skill. But the most important thing is not calculating that chart to perfection, it's finding companies, investing in them, and helping them grow. That's what makes or breaks your career in venture.

The other common myth is that you have to be the most technical person in the room to be successful in venture, which is simply not true. There is obviously a benefit to being the most technical person in the room; for example, being technical does help in figuring out the importance of the problem, timing, and market size because it is sometimes easier to iterate on these ideas yourself. It is easier to brainstorm and think about the market and timing based on your experience and be able to say, "This is my opinion of the market, this is the product I want to see that solves this problem." But you can't narrowly focus on that one attribute, technical expertise, as a requirement for success because the reality is every company is built with multiple different people. Every successful company needs at least one person with expertise in sales, in marketing, in technology, in product, and when a venture capitalist is investing in a company, they are putting on all those different hats. Relying on technical aspects of a company or giving that priority over all the other attributes and qualities that make a company successful is not a sure-fire recipe for success. You can also ask for help because nobody can be an expert in every area. I've seen so many instances where a venture capitalist asks a Chief Information Security Officer (CISO) friend, "Hey, CISO, can you evaluate this company? I would love your opinion on it." And the CISO comes back to the VC and says they hate it; it doesn't make any sense—and the VC will invest anyway. It's useful to get multiple different data points but that will take time and so sometimes leaning on your own experience allows you to move faster. Focusing on just one aspect, like technology, will not necessarily lead to the best decision.

In venture, we're taking on a risk and you do have to take a leap of faith. Sometimes having experience, or some parallel experiences that apply somewhat, will probably be enough to make a good decision. But no one knows the future, so we do have to take a risk. We just don't need to have the same skills, we don't need to have the same likes and dislikes about people or products or teams. We just don't.

There is another common misperception about venture, and that is that people with a particular personality type or people with specific characteristics will do well in venture. I haven't found that to be true. I can't look at the successful people in venture and conclude that, on the Myers-Briggs scale, they all fall in the same quadrant or that they all have the same strengths. Most people will leverage the strengths they have. So, a lot of Next-Gen VCs apply their financial strengths or their number analytical strengths; others apply their extroverted sales strengths, and being well liked is a strength; other people will apply their endurance, thinking that they'll just keep cranking and working 100-hour weeks; while some people love the networking dynamic of it. If I had to choose one factor that helps drive long-term success in this industry, and almost any career path, it is creativity and curiosity. That is especially important in environments like unstructured environments, such as venture capital. Even if you have a mentor, one mentor is not enough to understand the industry and move your career forward—maybe even two or three mentors are not enough. And finding a mentor can sometimes feel like a random chance. The most important attributes are curiosity and creativity and if you're not curious and you're not actively learning and growing, at some point, people are going to look at you and say, "Hey, why haven't you figured this out yet?"

12

Notes for Entrepreneurs
Some Thoughts

If you're looking from the outside in—you're an entrepreneur and you're ready to go get your first round of funding—the VC world can be intimidating. Hopefully this book will be a valuable tool in your arsenal, and you'll be able to walk people through the framework and land your financing. But I wanted to provide some nuances that can be helpful to entrepreneurs because as an entrepreneur, you need to go into it with an understanding of the overall strategy of the venture capital firm. Are you joining a family where you are one of 10 startups or are you joining a family where you're one of 100 startups? There is nothing wrong with either "family" and both of them make a ton of sense, but you just have to be very cognizant of what style of an investor you're talking to first. If you are an entrepreneur pitching to a VC where you're going to be in a cohort of 100, there is a lot of recognition by that VC firm that you might be a failure in the end for them. It will be okay for the VC because that VC has lots of other options, while you as the entrepreneur do not have many options.

The flip side in exchange for that higher risk that you take for working with a VC that has lots of startups in their portfolio is that they usually give you more room to run. They usually will give you more money or a higher valuation, but you are on your own. The other VC firm, where you are one of 10 startups, you know you are with a firm that wants to make sure every single one of those 10 startups becomes a success. You will not get terms as good as you would if you are in the larger firm, but since the smaller firm has fewer eggs, they will invest more time and provide more help to make you a success. So, as an entrepreneur, you need to figure out which style you prefer. Do you want help? Do you not want help? Do you want a hands-on VC or not?

So, if you're in a pitch meeting where you are one of 10 startups, where it's quality over quantity, those conversations are going to be very full of data and if you can, you should give them data across all these six factors in the VCIF that we talk about: the Who, What, When, Where, Why, and How. Because the more data they have, the more confidence they can build that they should put one of their very rare eggs with you. If you are working with an investor where you are one of 100 startups, they don't need all six. They can't process all that information and it's not reasonable for them to get data on all six factors at the same level and depth as the VC with 10 startups. The VC with 100 startups will usually focus on two or three of the six factors. But it depends on the stage. If you're an early-stage company, they will always value team. That's always really important. And then the second one they will value is usually either the problem or the market size.

For instance, if you think about Airbnb, they reimagined a category, let's say the B&B category, but the way they thought about it, it was a big total addressable market (TAM). What did the VCs prioritize there? What were the two most important things? If you wanted to be an early-stage investor in Airbnb, the most important quality was team, and the second was the size of the market. And if Airbnb found something that satisfied that market, that would make a huge difference. So those are the top two—team and market size. What was the third one? Maybe it is the problem, but not really, right? When early investors came into Airbnb, people were sleeping on air mattresses in your living room, they were sleeping on your couch. They didn't have the data to say, "Hey, this is what Airbnb is going to become." It was more likely, "Hey, invest in us. We are smart and we are tackling the travel industry, the hotel industry." And that was enough, right?

So when you work with a VC firm where you are one of a 100 startups, just recognize what the top three of the six factors are that they prioritize and really make sure that you're a good fit for those three factors. If you're working with a VC in a cohort of 100 and you are a later-stage company, team is actually not going to be the most important. It is important, of course, but the most important is the How. It's the organization that you've built so far, the metrics around customers, the sales and go-to market organizations, the technical team. And then what's the next most important? The next one is usually the solution. Is this a solution that generates positive feedback? Are customers giving you good feedback about the solution that the startup has built and are the numerical metrics good? Those are the top two. The third one is the team because at the end of the day, you have to work with a team. But, for a late-stage company, team is not the number one factor.

But now let's say you are working with a VC firm that does very few late-stage investments per year, and that firm is going to prioritize all six, they want to go deep everywhere. And usually—not always, but usually—the VC firms that prioritize all six have a greater hit rate of winners in terms of percentages, whether it's a better business model to do few investments or a better business model to prioritize all six, that is in the eye of the beholder. I don't know which one is better, but the percentage hit rate for late-stage investments is usually higher for a VC firm that has only a few investments versus a firm that does a 100 investments per year.

13

Notes for Startup Customers

Not every company has a mission to be a customer of a startup but those companies that do try to work with startups can create a win-win-win scenario. In my experience, I have seen at least two different versions of sophisticated customers that work with startups. One version is the global organization or category leader that is exceptionally good at rallying the people within their organization to both identify really interesting solutions or companies and deciding which projects that they want to take up. And then they also excel at collaborating with a startup so that it's a win-win for everyone. If the startup is early-stage, then the customer can ask for an incredibly great deal and lock in a great price for a very long time. One example of a sophisticated company that works with startups comes from a very early customer of VMware back when VMware was in its early days. Because this customer partnered early in VMware's development, they were able to lock in a ridiculous price for a very long time. That made the customer look great because the customer was then able to use the cost savings of working with VMware for other things, while demonstrating how innovative they were as an organization. And VMware also benefited because they got to talk about how they had this amazingly sophisticated early-adopter customer and how that customer helped them to find the roadmap. The customer got to help define their roadmap and also lock in a great price for a long time. So that's a win-win.

The second version of a startup customer that I have seen is the customer that enjoys working with startups because they believe in helping the creation process of a startup. In this scenario, I have found that, on the customer side, the person leading the charge is someone who's incredibly curious, or they want to be a founder themselves one day, or they really enjoy seeing someone make such a big leap in creating a business. It's a very brave decision to be an entrepreneur and there are some customers that want to support that creation in any way possible. There are also customers that want to be close to innovation because they really enjoy seeing the excitement, the buzz, the innovation of working with the startup as well.

This second startup customer is very much a customer who really likes that personal component of working with a startup. You don't often get that personal component a lot of times when you work with a big company with, for example, the sales reps in a large organization. But with a startup, you often can get that personal component. And this second version of a startup customer can do really well in terms of striking a good deal, they get the personal component, and they have an enjoyable experience. The startup benefits too because they get a committed customer very early— one who is often less concerned about the perfect product and more concerned about helping the startup develop and flesh out parts of its business model.

The third version of a customer that I've seen work really well with startups is the most tactical but also leads to a win-win outcome. The driver of the third scenario customer is that there are always problems that are not being solved by a large legacy platform company because problems evolve so quickly every single day. There are just scenarios that organizations face where you ask an incumbent to do something for you but they either can't or won't help solve your problem. The reality is that there are many, many problems out there and maybe the legacy company is not interested in this problem or maybe all their resources are invested in focusing in a different direction. So sometimes there is a very tactical and forceful reason why customers work with startups, because if a company has an urgent need that only the startup can solve, the company will work with the startup.

One of the best ways for this version of a customer to work with startups is to develop some internal processes that help the evaluation of potential startup partners. The process should include who is going to be the business owner, who is going to be the influencer, who is going to be the user, because without responsibilities and account-abilities, it will be easy for the startup to get lost within the larger organization, to have things delayed, or to provide a suboptimal solution.

The other dynamic that's really helpful in taking this kind of tactical decision, especially with a startup, is to look at the investors of the startup. It is not really intuitive until you've done many of these investments with a startup as a customer, but understanding who the investors are pays dividends for the tactical customer. When working with a lot of customers who have had experience purchasing from multiple startups, that's when tactical customers are able to more easily identify the signal, that's when they are able to differentiate the signal from the noise. And one of those important signals is from the investors who are betting on this startup. Of course, other parts of the VCIF come into play as well, like getting a good feel for the leaders of the startup. Are they people who you trust or should be trusted, based on their background?

Customers of startups come in three varieties, either working with them early to help define the roadmap and get superior long-term discounts, or embracing the entrepreneurial process and wanting to help usher that along, or needing a solution that only startups can help by solving their problem. All three of those customer profiles lead to a win-win and help to develop the entrepreneurial ecosystem.

14

Notes for LPs

Characteristics of Some of the Best VCs

Limited partners (LPs) play a critical role in venture capital and there is a lot of diversity in who these LPs are. For example, some folks have been investing in venture for a long time and have seen a lot, have been there for the ups and downs of markets, while others are just getting into investing in venture as a way to diversify their portfolios. But despite the diversity, one of the things I think that's common with LPs is that they often hire a consultant to help with due diligence and qualification of a VC firm. It's too much work, too specialized, and too nuanced for many LPs to figure out whether or not they should invest in a particular VC firm, so they often outsource that to a consulting firm like Cambridge Associates, for instance.

When I think about the diligence that an LP should do to evaluate a VC, the number one thing that is the most important—based on working with multiple other VCs in my career—is sector knowledge. Of course, there are a lot of dynamics that come into play and you can find a VC firm based on financial performance, or how good they are at sourcing, or how sophisticated they are at doing financial diligence and pricing, but to me the most important quality of a VC firm is sector experience. So, how would you apply the VCIF to understand VC firms and, in particular, sector knowledge? The VCIF can be applied to VC firms pretty well.

The Who is the VC team that an LP will invest in, the What is the sector—what is the problem and do you, as an LP, agree with the problem? The When is the timing, and you'll have to consider whether or not this is a great sector that is well-timed for success. The Where is the market—is this a large enough sector that can generate the outcomes that you're looking for? The Why is the solution, and you'll ask questions of VC firms around adequate solutions that can be built or have been built that will help resolve the problems within the industry. And the How gets at the execution—is there a critical mass of talent and knowledge that will allow great companies to be formed and scaled? So LPs looking to invest in venture can use the same VCIF framework to figure out, "Hey, I would like to work with this firm."

One thing I think about with some of the LPs I've really enjoyed working with is that the best ones, the most successful LPs, have had their own thesis about what spaces they want to invest in. Not only do they want to invest in venture capital, but they also want to invest within a specific sector within venture capital. And, in fact, the connection between having a thesis or preference for a space and success was validated by research by Cambridge Associates, where they showed that LPs have better returns if they invest in VCs with deep sector expertise versus generalists, especially in developed markets. Even if you have a well-developed thesis, there are many, many VC firms that might have expertise in the sector, so how do you figure out who to work with in a specific sector? To be able to evaluate VC firms on sector knowledge, you'll have to dig deeper and understand the level of expertise.

SECTOR KNOWLEDGE

Since LPs that invest in sectors are more likely to be successful, being able to carry out due diligence on VC firms to understand their sector expertise is a critical skill. I use a three-level framework to understand sector expertise and the labels for each level could be anything but for simplicity I just label them Level One, Level Two, and Level Three. I don't think Level One, Level Two, and Level Three means that a Level One investor is worse than a Level Three investor either. I just think that this is how you calibrate the level of their sector expertise. And so the question is, how do you know if a VC firm is at Level One, Level Two, or Level Three?

The Level One VC, in my opinion, is mostly a generalist who will opportunistically invest in a sector. It's actually quite common, and we see that all the time. For example, sometimes you see an enterprise investor investing in the security space, which is my area of expertise, or you see a FinTech investor investing in consumer. One way to figure out if a VC firm is a Level One is to ask them how they arrived at their thesis to invest in a sector. Do they understand the space based on their own research, by talking to analysts, or by talking to startups? A common theme that you'll see among folks who are Level One with sector expertise is that they actually get a lot of their knowledge about the spaces that they're focused on by speaking to startups. They are being educated by the startups that they're meeting and then, based on that information, they are forming a perspective on a specific sector. I won't say whether it's good or bad to be depending on startups to learn about a space, but that's the common theme that you'll see among folks who are out, who are at Level One of their sector expertise.

You can identify a Level Two VC by the amount of homework they have done. And what you'll find with a Level Two VC that you won't necessarily find with a Level One VC is that the Level Two person can name analysts, they can name the customers, and they can name the experts to whom they have spoken. They can talk about what those experts have told them and they can give you hypotheses based on what they've learned and heard from these different experts. Beyond that, when people get to this level, where they've done their homework, usually these are the VCs who have made more than two investments in the sector. So a Level Two VC has expertise that is both based on homework as well as real-world experience.

The highest level in terms of sector expertise is what I call a Level Three VC. What I really like about Level Three sector experts is that they are able to start drawing analogies. They can draw analogies from history, for instance, or from other industries and can say, "Oh, this happened in adtech and I think that trend is happening in FinTech." At Level Three expertise, a person not only starts to apply the data they have collected, but they can also understand why that data even exists and from there they can draw analogies to other industries or from history.

The other dynamic that you can see from people who are at this level of sector expertise is that they do start looking a little bit like a know-it-all. It's going to be very difficult to have a conversation with them where they don't at least have an opinion. Maybe they might not be an expert, maybe they don't know everything, maybe there is now a subcategory within the sector that is new, but they will at least have an opinion. And more importantly, they know exactly where to go to get the answers that they need.

A Level Three VC will have a network of folks that they know and they can tap into that knowledge. "Oh, you want to talk about data security? I know this person at this company, and they are so deep in data security that I will go talk to that person." A Level Three VC with sector knowledge not only has an opinion, but also has access to deep experts that you wouldn't be able to find through a service like Gartner or LinkedIn.

As an LP, you will most likely have a lot of options in choosing a VC and you may have a lot of well-respected consulting firms or experts advising you on VC firms as well, but you can use the VCIF framework to help narrow down the field. And once you do narrow down that field, you can focus on what I believe is the one key to prioritize: sector knowledge.

15

Long-Term Planning
Venture Capital Cycles, Optionality, Starting a VC firm

One of the changes that I've seen in venture capital is who is coming into the VC industry, who is joining. Not too long ago, the tried-and-true path to venture capital was someone who was a former founder or entrepreneur, typically a former CEO of a startup. Many of the people coming into venture in the past were people in their forties with direct entrepreneurial experience, but today we are seeing more and more people come in to venture without that startup background, and so my advice in this chapter is for the people considering venture as a career path who may be outsiders, like I was when I first started. Maybe you're thinking about a venture capital career but you don't know what to expect and if you want to be in venture, how do you do that if you don't have the CEO or startup pedigree?

When I talk to people early in their career, in high school, college, or just starting out, what I typically recommend that they do is to consider actually joining a startup and working for a startup. Since a lot of former founders or entrepreneurs become VCs, having that experience in a startup can be very helpful, especially if it's a successful startup.

If a startup is successful, that gives you the option to join yet another startup or potentially transition into venture capital. And then all the skills that you build at the startup will also be helpful if you decide to go join a big company. There are a lot of transferable skills that you can gain from working in a startup and that would be my first recommendation for most people who are interested in venture capital.

A second way to get into venture is to follow one of the three most common paths: investment banking, consulting, or sales. There is a reason behind each path. For example, someone with a sales background would be hired because a VC firm wants someone who can help them scale up their sourcing efforts, can outreach companies, and provide a great sense of how those companies are doing, so that the partners can get face-to-face time with them. The investment banking path might be the predominant one because VCs are looking for someone to help them do the financial analysis and the documentation of the deal, which are big tasks. And the consulting path is common because VCs need someone to help them build thought leadership or expertise in a specific space that they're interested in investing in. On top of that, a consultant can also help with the documentation and due diligence, too.

All three paths provide incredibly valuable optionality after college if you decide not to go into venture. For example, investment banking can lead to other financial positions like private equity or hedge funds; consulting can lead to communication strategy, and sales can be valuable to every business. But, the sales side is probably the most limiting because once you're in sales, people tend to want you to continue being in sales. It is a great career path but if you do choose the sales path, just make sure you have had some experience in sales beforehand. It doesn't matter if you worked at a company selling hotdogs, or books, or knives, or painting houses. But it's important to know whether or not you enjoy sales because it is a valuable skill set both in the entry-level part of the job and in the later stages of your job as you transition to becoming a partner or managing director. That's when you're expected to sell yourself and sell the firm as part of winning a deal. So, enjoying sales is almost a prerequisite to transitioning to the higher levels within a VC firm.

VENTURE CAPITAL CYCLES

One of the key dynamics that is critical to an understanding of venture is that venture capital comes in waves of interest. Although it might be really interesting right now, there is a very real possibility in a recessionary environment that venture capital will no longer be interesting, where people aren't finding jobs out of college—even prestigious colleges. Our whole world prioritizes stability. It prioritizes the highest possible cash salary, for example, and venture is risky. I would know because I graduated in a bad hiring market where people were valuing cash salaries, which is why I chose the investment banking path as a way to move into venture. But even when I was in investment banking, most people were seeking continued stability at a higher compensation level. And the firms that offer that are private equity firms, hedge funds, and even distressed debt investing.

Venture capital often gets lumped into a category with private equity, hedge funds, and investment banking but unlike those industries, venture has its waves of interest and it requires a lot of introspection in terms of why you're excited about venture capital. This book ought to help people with that introspection. For example, before you join a VC firm, it's very hard to know for certain if you're interested in venture capital as a career, because it's very hard to know what VCs do. It was hard for me, at least, because I didn't know what diligence was required to make an investment. I didn't know what criteria were important to do diligence on either. I didn't know about the different specializations. I didn't know about the different stages. All I knew when I started in venture was, hey, I have an entre-preneurial background and I love the power of creation, the power of building something out of nothing. I want a career that allows me to keep doing more of that, creating some-thing out of nothing.

When I was looking at this path of venture capital, at the same time I was actually looking at a path of joining a startup, of founding a company because that was another way of creating something out of nothing. In many ways I feel very lucky that I got a venture capital job because there weren't that many open slots when I was recruited, so when I thought about all of my options, I limited all my options to potential ways to create something out of nothing. What are the ways to enable creation? I still had backup plans and since I was in investment banking, I could join a private equity firm, or go into corporate finance, or go do mergers and acquisitions. The point is, I had a lot of options, and that is a key to creating a great career for yourself.

OPTIONALITY

The most important thing I think anyone should be pri-oritizing, especially earlier in their lives, is what I call optionality—the ability to build skills and experiences across many different industries and jobs. Of course, you have to balance that optionality with risk and reward. And part of that optionality is some introspection of understanding yourself and understanding why you want to pursue a particular career path, making sure that what you are excited by is aligned with this industry as well. One of the things I've noticed in successful careers is that success tends to require someone to specialize. What that means is usually you need to be known for something in order for people to give you attention. In the earliest days of your career, you are one of millions of people and as a result, people need some way of thinking of you or wanting to work with you. And the best way you do that is by specializing.

One way you can demonstrate some initial version of specializing is your major. For example, if you major in finance, then people will naturally think of you for finance jobs; if you major in computer science, you'll get those jobs, and so on. So there's a lot of value in choosing your major because that's your first way of showing specialization. That's your first way of demonstrating both the skills and the interests and these bring the jobs that people will recruit you for.

But while you're doing that specialization, I think the other part that's really important to think about is the likely path and to also map out what happens. If you take an engineering job out of college, what are the different paths after that? Probably the next path will be a manager of engineering teams. What's the next path after that? Okay, I decided to go get an MBA—fine, what's the next path after that as well? On one hand, the world forces you to specialize in order to be successful, but, on the other hand, you are responsible for your own career path. You are responsible for making sure that you have as many options as possible as well.

And it's a balancing act, right? If you come out of college and say, "I don't know what I want," no one will hire you. Or if you say the opposite, that you want to do "everything," no one will hire you either. And if you come out of college and say, "I only want to do one thing," the number of job opportunities will be limited but you're also very likely to get that job because you know exactly what you want. One thing to think about is choosing a career path that doesn't have very long legs, doesn't keep going for a long period of time, or growth opportunities are limited. For example, suppose you decide to become a pilot and the way that works is you start as a co-pilot in a commuter airline, then become a captain of a commuter airline, then try to get a job with a major airline. You'll start as a co-pilot but eventually you can become a captain. But then what? Both the growth and advancement opportunities are limited because once you become a captain, there's nothing else. And, airlines face challenges that could impact you, like bad years where you're furloughed, or moved to a smaller airplane. So, especially early in your career, you do have to be very mindful of options.

Every person has the responsibility of making sure they prioritize optionality on their own end, and what happens over time, as you become more and more successful, is that you have more options and those options will only get better over time. When you think about people who are so successful that they become millionaires or billionaires or whatever metric you use to define "success," when they have financial freedom they can do whatever they want. They can make their wealth in oil and decide to go buy a basketball team, for example.

When we think about optionality and venture, one thing that is characteristic of venture is that not every single person who starts in the VC career path becomes a partner or managing director of a VC firm. You have to think about optionality if you do decide to pursue a VC career path because one of the downsides of venture capital, in my opinion, is that there actually isn't optionality after you have a venture capital career. A lot of the skills that you build are not easily transferred. The most transferable place for venture skills is a finance version of a venture capital path. For example, you can transfer venture skills into corporate development where you're taking the diligence skills that you used as a VC and applying that diligence to acquiring startups or acquiring companies. Another skill that can be transferred is sales, where maybe you find great companies, convince them to work with you, and then you convert that into an investment banking job where you help find great companies for the investment bank. Overall, the reality is that there is not a multitude of great paths after you participate in venture, so you have to be really, really mindful of that as well.

Where do VCs go if they haven't achieved success at the highest levels in their careers? I've seen some VCs go back to engineering because they had an engineering background. I've seen some go into operational roles like chief of staff or COO. I've seen some go into corporate development, and some go into sales and business development. The one dynamic people need to know is that when you do work in the venture capital role and you transition into a functional role, people tend to ask you to do startup-related things. It's likely, for instance, that you will take an operational role at a startup or a finance role at a startup. And so people who leave venture are somewhat locked into the startup ecosystem. If you value working at Microsoft and one day hopefully becoming an executive vice president (EVP) at Microsoft, it's important to note that it's a very, very long path to go from a venture capital career to becoming an executive at a big tech company. It's possible, but it requires a lot of pivots to make that happen.

One path I haven't discussed is the true outsider path. Suppose you have a liberal arts degree from a small school and you'd like to know, is the venture capital career an option for me? When I think about entry level or up-and-coming VCs, the key thing to always recognize is that there is a certain amount of work that needs to get done but can't get done because there's only so much time or attention a partner can give to be able to manage multiple things. When they hire an entry-level VC, they are hiring that person to take over things they just don't have the time to do. If you're a true outsider, the first thing to do is identify those things that can be delegated to an entry-level VC and then, second, build those skills and demonstrate that you can take over those responsibilities and execute on them incredibly well.

Early in any career, everyone is expected to invest in themselves and if you're not willing to invest in yourself, why should someone else invest in you? This is especially true for a VC, which is very much a mentorship-driven industry. It is possible to go to any college and major in anything and build these skills and demonstrate that you are a great person to delegate certain responsibilities to. If you're reading this book, this is an investment and the book is a way of helping you decide whether you want to get on the venture capital path. If you understand the framework in which VCs make investing decisions, that provides you knowledge of the industry before you get involved, and once you get into venture, it helps you build the skills and the confidence that you need to be able to find ways to help a senior investor or a partner augment those responsibilities as well.

COULD YOU START YOUR OWN VC FIRM?

You might be wondering if creating your own VC firm is an option. Of course, if you do have money from friends or family or maybe a startup exit, you have more options and you could start investing yourself. That's great, and there are platforms like AngelList that allow you to start seeing companies and invest into startups. If your goal is to create your own portfolio and then leverage that to demonstrate that you're a good investor so that you can get a VC firm to hire you, that is a very difficult path. It's actually a very uncommon path, even though a lot of people want to enter venture that way, but it's very rare. And one reason why it's not a path to venture when you do it all by yourself, you invest based on your research, and you are learning by yourself, you can start learning some lessons the wrong way. And that requires the next person who hires you to teach you to unlearn those lessons and relearn some important lessons. And that is very difficult and, in some cases, might be more work to help someone unlearn and relearn than to just start with a person who doesn't know anything.

Beyond learning the wrong things, one of the dynamics of the venture industry is that the institutional firms, with hundreds of millions or billions of dollars in a fund, invest very differently than someone who has $10 million. When you are investing your own money and you're writing (relatively) small checks, you don't get a board seat at a startup. You don't get all the information and therefore you don't get to do all the diligence that you want to do. You're not learning all the skills that are relevant for a larger fund because the larger firms have to source and find investments differently than an angel investor would, and a larger firm will diligence companies differently. A large VC firm will have a responsibility to their own investors as LPs, and then they also have the responsibility to the companies as board members. Those are all gigantic sets of skills that are very difficult to cultivate if you are an independent angel investor.

The only short-cut to venture, and I wouldn't recommend it, is to find your way onto a company board, especially a board that includes other experienced investors, because you learn a lot by being on a board and you get a lot of visibility on why people make the decisions that they make on a strategic level as a board member. I'm saying that as a short-cut, not as a tried-and-true method to get into venture. It might happen that a person gets a board seat because of a favor from a CEO or founder who finds someone so incredibly helpful to them and they have such confidence in them that they want to expose that person to their board. But, this path is very uncommon and, honestly, there are a lot of contingencies and difficulties to overcome.

The most realistic path to venture if you can't pursue one of the traditional paths that I mentioned before as an entry-level person, is being a founder or an executive at a startup. And this path works because as a founder or executive, you at least get visibility into the board meetings, you will learn exactly how to add value as a board member, and you will get the ability to build skills that are really valuable to becoming an investor.

Conclusion

I first coined a catchphrase I use all of the time, "Everyone is an investor" or "We are all investors," back in 2018. At that time, I was several years into my venture capital career, and while I was simultaneously figuring out how VCs made investing decisions, I was also figuring out why customers made purchasing decisions. And that's when I eventually realized how much of life was a series of investment decisions.

And I am not alone in that thinking. Whether it's the family huddled over their breakfast table calculating paychecks and bills, or the college student pondering their first full-time job, or the millions of people trying to figure out 401(k)s and workplace stock options, or the person deciding if they should rejoin the workforce after years, everyone is making investments all the time. Whether it's explicitly stated or written down by a person or left as an idea, everyone is producing hypotheses and betting largely on guesses about the future that they see. What drives those decisions? How do we, consistently, make sure that our hypotheses and bets lead to more winners than losers at the investment table?

In this book I have looked at the issue of how people make decisions in the largely opaque venture capital industry and,

over years of thinking, listening to others, and experimenting on my own, I have been able to create a framework that
works for me and will work for you, too. The puzzle of how
VCs make decisions gnawed at me both personally and pro-
fessionally as I pursued a more traditional and direct life in
the world of investments with a career in venture capital.
And what happened for me was that I eventually discovered
that there is structure in how VCs make decisions, it's just
not explicitly articulated as a complete framework. The Venture Capital Investment Framework (VCIF) is my attempt
at putting structure into the VC decision-making process to
help people understand venture capital and be successful in
it. On your own, without a mentor, without a framework,
without some guiding ideas, any hypothesis you come up
with may lead you to believe that you don't have enough
understanding of the data to place a bet, or you don't know
if you're even looking at the most relevant data to help you
make a decision. The VCIF is a way to help you take a vast
amount of information and be able to hone it down into siz-
able buckets, to place data into categories that make sense
and lead to better decisions.

My hope is that *The VC Field Guide* will help people overcome some of that lack of data and that you can use the
framework to ask the right questions. But it's only a starting point, not an end point. You can use my framework as
a way to build your own framework, you can add to it or
take some of the components away. I didn't write this as a
definitive solution for all time, but as a guide for how VCs
currently think about investing in startups and why they
make the decisions that they do.

One of the things that I feel strongly about, and I wrote
about it in several different parts of the book, is the idea of
specialization and how people who specialize early in their
career can develop skills that catapult them to the top of

their niche. VC firms also specialize in sectors or markets and that can be a huge benefit to an entrepreneur looking for funding because you'll be able to figure out more quickly if the VC you're talking to can continue to add value to you and your team. It's also possible, if you're a Next-Gen VC, or you're in an investment club, or you have a family that likes to invest together, that you can specialize and focus on just one component of the framework and then share your findings and ideas with others. One person might become an expert on evaluating teams, one on timing, and one on scale, for example, and when you get together, you can then share what you've learned on your own with everyone else. It's the divide and conquer approach, and rather than try to do everything yourself, you can lean on (and learn from) your colleagues.

The venture industry is impactful and exciting and I hope this book helps people all over the world build businesses. While the startup world can seem so fast-moving, the reality is that things take time, especially with entrepreneurship and innovation, because you need skills, networks, confidence, capital accessibility, and like-minded people to create an entrepreneurial ecosystem. It takes a village to build a startup and that's one reason why Silicon Valley is so powerful. It has everything from training people in colleges and universities, to the critical mass of entrepreneurs learning from each other, working with each other and becoming successful, and then those people turning their capital into investments for future entrepreneurs. There's an ecosystem component to Silicon Valley, but it's not limited to Silicon Valley—it's growing all over the world. And one of the ways that's possible is because knowledge is being shared more freely. There are more books being written, more videos being shared, more boot camps being offered.

And so it is possible to be able to start anywhere. It's just that when you build a startup in an ecosystem, you are limited to the resources in your community. I understand that many founders and entrepreneurs aspire to be remote-first, but many times people have to hire locally so there's still a regional component to how we work—no matter how hard we try to get away from that. There are language barriers or even time zone differences so entrepreneurship still requires a talent base to support it, it requires people, with each one individually growing. At some point a company needs a director of marketing, at some point the company needs a VP of marketing, at some point they need a CMO. And we need talent available to fill each of those roles and that is why it takes time to build a vibrant, robust ecosystem like Silicon Valley.

But if you like to be close to creation, if you like to help ideas become a reality, if you want to impact founders and employees and customers and communities, then venture is a way to do that. And if you want to do that well, then asking the right questions and looking at the right data will help you be successful in that. The Venture Capital Investment Framework is a tool that can be valuable to people in, and outside of, venture capital.

Afterword

I've always been fascinated by the power of venture capital as a loudly revving engine behind technology innovation, life-altering inventions, and economic growth. During the course of my 20-year career documenting the tectonic shifts and business patterns in enterprise technology, the VC model has been on display front and center, introducing new entrepreneurs, new ideas, new companies, and new product categories.

Like many, I've sometimes struggled to understand some VC investments and big-money decisions. Any attempt at deciphering this world was filled with marketing-speak and techno-babble, leading to active skepticism and a general misunderstanding of the world of venture capital.

As I close the pages of this remarkable field guide, my mind drifts back to an earlier chat I had with Will and his "everyone's an investor" approach to simplifying investment conversations.

It's pretty startling how perfectly Will's investment framework merges seamlessly with the more familiar principle of the Five Ws and, as a hardcore sports fan, the player-coach relationship connections helped add clarity to a very nuanced space.

This book was more than just a treatise on venture capital decision-making. I found it to be a guidebook for many important parts of life, providing important lessons (from hardened experience) on the importance of empathy, values, building strong relationships, and constantly questioning and modifying our own hypotheses.

As I raced through this field guide, I found myself highlighting passages, taking notes, and discussing the framework with newsroom colleagues. I'm already using the framework in my own data-mapping projects tracking the cybersecurity startup landscape. The guide has turned into a template for connecting the micro to the macro, for looking beyond the surface to see patterns around timing, TAM, and scale.

I now have a deeper understanding of how VCs pinpoint good (and problematic) founders, how teams are put together, how market categories are created, how sustainable businesses are scaled, and how first principles are applied in a structured way.

In short, this guide was a revelation and I've found myself reaching for it time and time again as a reference and a source of guidance for my work.

Ryan Naraine
Editor-at-Large, *SecurityWeek*
Podcast host, SecurityConversations.com

Glossary

A Player: Qualitative rating system to differentiate qualities of team members with A as the highest rating, followed by B, C, D.

A Team: Qualitative grading system to measure teams with A as the highest rating.

ACV: Annual contract value. Metric used in venture capital to measure bookings on a 12-month basis.

ARR: Annual recurring revenue. A metric used to measure subscription-based revenue on a 12-month basis.

BYOD: Bring your own device. A movement within companies where employees could work using their own personal devices.

Carry: The percentage of the investment profits that a venture capital fund keeps. Also called carried interest.

CFO: Chief Finance Officer.

CISO: Chief Information Security Officer also commonly called CSO, Chief Security Officer.

CMO: Chief Marketing Officer.

COO: Chief Operating Officer.

CRM: Customer relationship management.

CRO: Chief Revenue Officer.

CTO: Chief Technology Officer.

Ecosystem: A term applied to all the participants in an organization or system, who are connected in some way.

Entrepreneurial ecosystem: All the people, companies, and institutions involved in entrepreneurship, from entrepreneurs, to vendors, customers, venture capitalists, financial institutions, universities, to all the employees and anyone else involved in entrepreneurship and innovation.

European waterfall: A structure where the VC fund only receives carried interest after the limited partners have had returned all of their invested capital.

Fortune 500: A list of the 500 largest by revenue publicly traded companies in the United States.

GAAP: Generally accepted accounting principles.

GP: General Partner. An employee of the venture capital firm who invests capital in the funds that the firm manages.

GP commitment: The amount of capital the General Partners of a venture capital firm collectively commit to invest personally in a venture capital fund. Typically expressed as a percentage of the fund size.

IPO: Initial public offering. The process of offering shares of a private corporation to the public by issuing new publicly-tradable stocks.

KPI: Key performance indicators. Metrics used to measure various corporate functions separately.

LBO: Leveraged buyout. A financial technique where the acquiring company raises debt to acquire a target company.

LP: Limited Partner. An outside investor who invests in funds for the purposes of financial returns. LPs can be very large institutions like pension funds, non-profits, corporations, or individuals.

M&A: Mergers and Acquisitions. A financial technique where companies are acquired and consolidated.

Next-Gen VC: A person early in their venture capital career.

Pattern matching: Taking prior experiences or learning and applying them to a new situation.

Returning the fund: A term that describes a successful investment or activity that returns all of the capital invested in a fund and brings a fund into paying carried interest, if not already doing so.

ROI: Return on investment. A measure of performance for companies where the return of the investment is measured based on the cost of the investment.

Rule of 40: A metric that uses profitability (typically measured by EBITDA %) and growth (typically measured by Revenue % growth year-over-year) to evaluate a company. If those two values add up to 40 or greater, the company passes.

SAAS: Software as a service. A widely used business model where software is also hosted and delivered by the software provider rather than installed on company computers or servers. Also called on-demand or web-based.

Seed-stage company: The earliest stages of a startup, typically with a small founding team, an idea, and a vision. May or may not have customers or revenues but has seed funding.

Series A company: An early-stage startup having already raised a Series A round of capital. These companies typically have less than $1 million in revenues.

Series B company: An early-stage startup having already raised a Series B round of capital. These companies typically have more than $1 million in revenues and some traction in the market.

SMS: Short message service.

TAM: Total addressable market. The largest number of potential customers for a service, which provides a sense of the size of the opportunity.

TCV: Total contract value. A metric used to measure all the revenue a customer contract brings over all the years of the contract.

Unicorn: A term used to describe startups with valuations above $1 billion.

Utilization rate: A productivity measure used to evaluate how much of the total time an employee works is focused on customer-billable work.

Valuation: A quantitative process to determine the fair value of an asset.

VC: Venture capitalist or venture capital industry, depending on the context.

VCIF: Venture Capital Investment Framework. The Who, What, When, Where, Why, and How questions that are used by venture capitalists to make investment decisions.

Venture capital: An investment approach where funds are used to fund startup opportunities.

Venture capital firm: A holding company within venture capital that employs every person, including investors and operational roles.

Venture capital fund: A pool of capital raised by the firm for the purposes of investment by the firm. The capital is raised from general partners and limited partners.

Vintages: An annual time period used to compare venture funds raised in the same calendar year, since markets evolve and change.

Index